Praise for

for
lovers
of god
everywhere

"The first language of all mystics is poetry. Theologians camp way down stream from the source. They do for mystics what literary critics do for secular poets: not much. Roger Housden guides us upstream past the camps of theological schools to the valley of springs. Thus this book is a marvelous gift for all whose hearts yearn for God, as the deer yearns for living waters."
— **Brother David Steindl-Rast, OSB,**
co-founder of **www.gratefulness.org**

"I hope Roger Housden's wonderful work keeps reaching thousands, and helps to lift our world's wing and heart."
— **Daniel Ladinsky**, international best-selling
Penguin author of poetry

"Roger Housden has done it again—provided us with a cornucopia of spiritual wonders, explained and commented on with elegance and wit and a clarity illumined by the wisdom of fervor. This celebration of the Christian Mystical Tradition will exhaust and feed the souls of seekers on all paths."
— **Andrew Harvey**, author of *The Hope*

"Like luminous pools of still water, each of the poems that Roger has so skillfully selected casts light on the path of practice and quenches the spiritual thirst of sincere speakers. Roger's comments cast a pebble into these pools that stirs ripples of imagery and appreciation, enlivening their offering."
— **Paul Haller**, co-abbot, San Francisco Zen center

for
lovers
of god
everywhere

for
lovers
of god
everywhere

Poems of the Christian Mystics

ROGER HOUSDEN

HAY HOUSE, INC.
Carlsbad, California • New York City
London • Sydney • Johannesburg
Vancouver • Hong Kong • New Delhi

Published and distributed in the United States by: Hay House, Inc.: www.hayhouse.com •
Published and distributed in Australia by: Hay House Australia Pty. Ltd.: www.hayhouse
.com.au • **Published and distributed in the United Kingdom by:** Hay House UK, Ltd.: www
.hayhouse.co.uk • **Published and distributed in the Republic of South Africa by:** Hay House SA
(Pty), Ltd.: www.hayhouse.co.za • **Distributed in Canada by:** Raincoast Books: www.raincoast
.com • **Published in India by:** Hay House Publishers India: www.hayhouse.co.in

Design: Bryn Starr Best

Library of Congress Cataloging-in-Publication Data

Housden, Roger.
  For lovers of God everywhere : poems of the Christian mystics / Roger Housden. -- 1st ed.
      p. cm.
  ISBN 978-1-4019-2387-7 (trade pbk. : alk. paper) 1. Christian poetry. 2. Mysticism--
Poetry. 3. Mysticism in literature. I. Title.
  PN6110.R4H66 2009
  808.81'93823--dc22   2009021928

ISBN: 978-1-4019-2387-7

1st edition, November 2009
1st digital printing, January 2015

Printed in the United States of America

contents

introduction

If you want to speak of the ineffable and the essential, there is no better medium than poetry. Poetry is the language of the spirit and the soul, not of the discursive mind. It compresses the lived truth of the poet's experience into a beauty and wisdom that can slip under the skin of the reader and enter their bloodstream. When you don't know what to say you cry out, and those cries are the beginning of poetry. They are language informed not only by the mind but by the body and heart as well. Poetry is the language of choice for mystics in all traditions who have tried to communicate their insights and experiences for the benefit of those who will listen.

This collection of 98 poems from the Christian mystical tradition is for lovers of God everywhere, because lovers of God are everywhere, whatever their race or creed may be. More specifically, this book is for the mystics among us of any religion or none, those who put their faith less in external belief systems or dogma than in the more interior, personal experience of God and of existence itself. But the deeper and more interior these spiritual experiences become, the more universal they also tend to be, expressions of a common stream that feeds humanity and all its religions everywhere, no matter how different we may appear on the surface. That stream emerges in every tradition as the language of silence beyond thought, of longing and ecstasy, of a wisdom that can see beyond the limitations of forms and beyond language itself. Ultimately, it emerges in a celebration of union—the union on this earth and in this body of the human with the divine. This is the true spiritual marriage, the consummation of love that in one way or another is the aim of every ritual and every practice in every religion.

These are universal themes, and they sparkle and lace their way through the centuries of Christian history just as they do in Islam, Buddhism, Hinduism, and all the other great traditions. In the West, it all started with the Desert Fathers—the contemplative communities who went out into the Egyptian desert to find silence and solitude in the early centuries after the death of Jesus. Later, the practice extended into Europe through the formation of the monastic orders, but over time these became rule bound and more often bastions of church dogma than havens of personal contemplation. Christian mystics down through the ages have largely acted on the margins of the church, because subjective experience doesn't count when there's a one-dogma-for-all policy to uphold.

This is why many Christian mystics, to this day, remain relatively unknown to Christians. If you are building an international organization, you want a generally recognized chain of command and a mission statement that applies to everyone. The church struggled for centuries to formulate and declare a doctrine to be adhered to throughout the Christian world, and personal revelations were suspect because they bypassed dogma and formal teachings as well as the authority of the clergy. You can't have people voicing personal revelations that might bring down the whole house of cards. This is why so many of the great Christian mystics—Meister Eckhart and John of the Cross, to name but two—were always running the risk of heresy and death at the hands of the Inquisition. Others, like Marguerite Porete, were burned at the stake for speaking or writing of their revelations, while entire esoteric communities, like the Cathars, were exterminated.

Instead of encouraging personal revelation through mystical experience, the monastic orders emphasized daily work and the communal liturgy, which tended to keep everyone in line and on the same page, and it exalted the community over the individual. It may be surprising how many practicing Christians there are who have never heard of Meister Eckhart or Julian of Norwich, not to mention Pseudo-Dionysius; but in fact it could hardly be otherwise. For centuries, the church has maintained a great divide between its orthodox body of teachings and the writings of its mystics, whose revelations are almost never mentioned in church circles outside of the few who pursue a contemplative practice of their own.

This book exists to bring the beauty and wisdom of these Christian poets to a broader audience. The Christian mystical tradition is as rich, varied, and inspiring as any to be found on earth. Despite the dangers of incurring the wrath of the authorities, Christian contemplatives have, for two thousand years, given us humble yet soaring and ecstatic accounts of their experiences, visions, and intuitions on their path to union with God. Some, like Saint Teresa of Ávila, have mapped out the whole journey for us, so that we may follow in their footsteps. Others, like the anonymous English author of *The Cloud of Unknowing*, give us markedly different advice to follow. Teresa provides a detailed account of what she calls The Interior Castle of the Soul—the different rooms and experiences of which represent the stages of the soul's union with Christ the beloved. The English author tells us that God is unknowable and that we must follow the light of our own faith into the cloud of that unknowing.

Whichever way a particular individual's temperament led them, whether toward ecstatic visionary revelation or toward a deepening silence beyond any thought or image, the desired end of union was and is always the same. In the Christian tradition, these two mystical orientations were called respectively the via positiva, typified here by saints like Teresa of Ávila, Catherine of Siena, and Augustine, and the via negativa, represented by mystics like Pseudo-Dionysius, Meister Eckhart, and John Tauler. Though I could have divided the collection accordingly, or by a variety of sub-themes, I have chosen not to categorize the subject matter at all. I like the way this spontaneous juxtaposition brings different perspectives and sensibilities up against each other and the way it can set off surprising connections between poems with apparently different outlooks. I also like how it leaves the reader free to open the book at random and find her own favorites without being guided by some predetermined structure.

A mystic, or contemplative, aspires to union, though not with some entity in the sky, but with what is already the very ground of their own being, itself unnamable and forever beyond the grasp of the rational mind. There is nothing to acquire or add on to who we are; rather, the contemplative's attentive silence represents a turning toward his true nature. Christ is within, and the union or marriage with Christ is a surrender of the personal will and ego to our deepest and most essential humanness, both intimately personal and transpersonal at the same time. Since the personal will cannot help us on this journey, we can feel we are on the road without a map.

At the beginning of his great work The Ascent of Mount Carmel, John of the Cross gives a line drawing of what his book will be about. He sketches a mountain, symbol of the soul, and not far from the base he writes, "Here there is no longer any way because for the just man there is no law; he is a law unto himself." He means, not that we can do just as we like but that the realm of silence and stillness is, by its very nature, unchartable. All we can carry into it is the purity and clarity of our intention—our longing for God—along with a keen attentive awareness. These are the mystic's tools, his chalice and sword—the only qualities that can help him steer through his own delusions, illusions, and torpor.

Mysticism and its contemplative practices continue to exist in Christianity, as in every religious tradition, because they represent the intrinsic human desire to return to the source of our humanity. As Saint Augustine said in *The City of God,* "we must fly to our beloved homeland. There the Father is, and there is everything." In many ways the climate today is more encouraging of contemplative practices than it has been for centuries. Christians have no reason now to be afraid of challenging official church doctrine or of following their own personal and direct relationship with God. And with the globalization of religions, with secularization and democratization, contemplative practices that were previously hidden behind monastery doors are now commonplace activities among lay people.

Thomas Merton, among other Christian contemplatives, has pointed to the value for Christians of Buddhist meditation techniques, which have much in common—especially their emphasis on mindfulness, or watchfulness—with the advice of the early Desert Fathers, of the anonymous author of *The Cloud of Unknowing,* with Meister Eckhart, Hadewijch the Beguine, and others. At its best, this kind of cross-cultural pollination serves to remind us of the jewels that have been in our own backyard all along. It highlights just how much insight and wisdom there really is in the work of these Christian mystics, whose work has, for so long, been deemed obscure at best and heretical at worst.

Even more, the recent and highly popular translations of the poetry and sayings of the Sufi mystics, Rumi and Hafez, and of the Hindus, Mirabai and Kabir, have given renewed impetus to the language and way of love and union with God. The Sufi Muslim and the Hindu mystics share with Christianity the notion of a personal God, and these poets have brought fresh inspiration and appreciation for the poetry of devotion to the Christian Western world.

Today, Rumi's poetry is far better known in the West than that of Angela of Foligno, Teresa of Ávila, Catherine of Siena, or any number of other great Christian voices. Yet the words of these Christian saints are equally inspired and inspiring as those of the Sufi from Konya in Turkey. What Rumi's popularity has done, along with that of Hafez and others, is to help prepare the ground for the re-emergence of the great poetic and spiritual voices of our own Christian tradition. The Sufis and the Hindus are reminding us that we too have our great love songs to God, our cries of longing, our sorrows of separation, our bliss of union. These are perennial and timeless, and this current collection exists to celebrate these voices in the Christian tradition; universal voices that transcend sectarian divides and speak to the heart of our humanity.

If our times are more open to contemplative practices than earlier eras, it will not be surprising to find the work of contemporary poets in this volume alongside that of figures from the Middle Ages or from the very beginnings of Christianity. Christian contemplatives today may be found in almost any life circumstance, not just in the monastery. And in our current cultural context, I wouldn't even call them contemplatives. The spiritual life has become democratized and secularized. What might have once been called contemplative living might now be more aptly described as giving primary value to the interior life, of developing a spiritual sensibility within the secular world in which we live.

A life of seclusion is no longer necessary for this; although periods of personal retreat have become a common practice for many. The inner life may be the priority of a psychologist, a poet, a writer, a medical practitioner, or a craftsman—of anyone in any occupation. So while Mary Oliver, for example, whose poem Praying ends this collection, may not see herself as a mystic or a contemplative, she is certainly a Christian who gives primary value to the inner life and whose poems spring from that source. In that sense, she is part of the long lineage of Christian poets stretching back to John of the Cross and beyond. So too is Mark Jarman, even if—especially if—the poem of his that begins the collection starts with the lines:

Drunk on the Umbrian hills at dusk and drunk
on one pink cloud that stood beside the moon,

For weren't Saint Francis of Assisi , Saint Teresa of Ávila, and St John of the Cross all drunk on a wine they had no name for? Wasn't a wine of rare vintage the very draught that Rumi and Hafez and Mirabai sang the praises of too? This is the real point of this book: that you too may catch the scent and savor of that wine and develop a taste for it that prompts you to pick up these glorious poems and read them aloud to yourself or a loved one as part of your daily nourishment. As Derek Walcott said, in his poem "Love After Love":

Give wine. Give bread. Give back your heart
to itself, to the stranger who has loved you

all your life.

These poems are a spoon for that kind of feast.

poems of the christian mystics

Unholy Sonnet 13

Drunk on the Umbrian hills at dusk and drunk
On one pink cloud that stood beside the moon,
Drunk on the moon, a marble smile, and drunk,
Two young Americans, on one another,
Far from home and wanting this forever—
Who needed God? We had our bodies, bread,
And glasses of a raw, green, local wine,
And watched our Godless perfect darkness breed
Enormous softly burning ancient stars.
Who needed God? And why do I ask now?
Because I'm older and I think God stirs
In details that keep bringing back that time,
Details that are just as vivid now—
Our bodies, bread, a sharp Umbrian wine.

— Mark Jarman

This gorgeous poem by Mark Jarman, a professor of English and respected American poet, manages to bring heaven and earth together in

Our bodies, bread, a sharp Umbrian wine.

It's not only the lovers who are expressions of God here—the whole world, we can assume, is shot through with light, if only our eyes are open to seeing. Wine and bread are the sacraments of the communion, the point of which is to be gathered up in love; so Jarman's jaunt with his beloved on an Umbrian hillside becomes, with the benefit of hindsight, a communion with all Creation, a wedding party for the Lord.

———◆———

Drink My Wine

Jesus said,

Drink my wine
you will become me
I will become you
and all that is hidden
you will see
with your own eyes.

— Logion 108, The Gospel of Thomas

Drink the wine and the scales will fall from your eyes and you will see as Christ-in-you sees. But what is the wine? The words of Jesus, which, when truly heard, become a transforming nectar for the hungry soul? The awareness, by grace, of the presence of Christ in you? In whatever form it comes, Communion means that a new life enters your bloodstream and the truth that is most hidden can be revealed: you are not, and never were, on your own. You are always and ever joined to the Source, one with the All. The Gospel of Thomas, part of the apocryphal literature of the years soon after the death of Jesus, is at times oblique, even opaque, but this verse shines like a lamp.

———◆———

The Sky's Sheets

When He touches me I clutch the sky's sheets,
the way other
lovers
do

the earth's weave
of clay.

Any real ecstasy is a sign
you are moving
in the right
direction,

don't let any prude tell
you otherwise.

— Saint Teresa of Ávila

Orgasmic realizations will always be frowned upon by those who feel they have to keep up appearances. Get used to it! Saint Teresa of Ávila, friend and contemporary of Saint John of the Cross, was one of the most ecstatic lovers ever to have emerged in the Christian tradition. Her goal was spiritual marriage with Christ, the mere thought of which would make her soul faint with joy. In Ladinsky's rendering, Teresa's words are vigorous, contemporary, and in this case, raunchily humorous. But Teresa was a woman of the world as well as a contemplative and known not only for her mystical visions, ecstasies, and raptures but also for her reforms of the Carmelite Order and her courage, ebullience, and humor in the face of Church authority.

———◆———

Song: If You Seek . . .

Follow my ways and I will lead you
To golden-haired suns,
Logos and music, blameless joys,
Innocent of questions
And beyond answers:
For I, Solitude, am thine own self:
I, Nothingness, am thy All.
I, Silence, am thy Amen!

— *Thomas Merton*

In the spaciousness of silence, empty of thoughts and preoccupations, of questions and answers, a different world can emerge, a world of deep beauty and peace. There are many ways to that silent land, but for Thomas Merton, the personal God, or Christ, is the One who leads him there.

Merton, one of the first Christian monastics to explore the common ground in the contemplative practices of different traditions, goes directly to the core here with his assertion that No-thingness and Silence are the All and the Amen. He wrote much in his journals of his affinity for Buddhism, and his writings on solitude and silence have been a significant influence on Christian contemplative practice since the 1950s. Merton was a member of the Christian via negativa tradition, which stretches back almost two thousand years and focuses on No-thingness and Silence, qualities often associated exclusively with Buddhism.

————◆————

The Untamed (excerpt)

the silence
Holds with its gloved hand
The wild hawk of the mind.

— R.S. Thomas

R.S. Thomas, a clergyman whose parish was in rural Wales, drew many of his images from the country life and ways of the people he lived among. I love this single image. It captures so beautifully the relation between silence and the ordinary mind, our customary identity. The falconer wears a leather glove for his falcon to perch on before releasing it to seek its prey. Without the glove the falcon could harm the falconer's hand. I like to think that the glove is our attention, which protects the silence. With our attention, the silence can hold "the wild hawk of the mind" and prevent it from running off on its own flights of fancy. The mind is indeed wild, and resting our attention in silence is part of its taming, or training.

———◆———

You are the mystery (excerpt)

> you are the mystery that
> is placed upon the Lord's table.
> You receive the mystery that is
> yourself.
> To that which you are,
> you will respond,
> 'Amen.'

> — Saint Augustine

This is the good news: we are already the one we are looking for. Augustine says as much in these lines drawn from his homily on the Feast of Pentecost. Pentecost, or Whitsunday, was when the Holy Spirit descended in tongues of fire on the disciples who were gathered with Jesus in the Upper Room—the scene of the Last Supper. They were infused with the Spirit of God, as we are too, which the rite of the Eucharist serves to remind us.

In placing ourselves on "the Lord's table," we are offering up our familiar identity and receiving in its place the body of Christ, which, in truth, is who we already are. We are already one with God in our Christ nature. As we experience this, the word 'Amen' will fall from our lips, for it literally means "It is so," or "This is the truth."

———◆———

Holy Spirit

Holy Spirit,
giving life to all life,
moving all creatures,
root of all things,
washing them clean,
wiping out their mistakes,
healing their wounds,
you are our true life,
luminous, wonderful,
awakening the heart
from its ancient sleep.

— Hildegard of Bingen

Hildegard was a Renaissance woman some 400 years before the Renaissance. You name it, she did it: music, visions, books on natural history and medicine, abbess of a monastery, and more. Her voice will last forever. In this poem it falls like a stream from one image to the next and showers upon us the benediction of the Holy Spirit, who dissolves our mistakes and washes us clean, who wakens us from the sleep of Ages.

———◆———

Draw me after You!

Draw me after You!
We will run in the fragrance of Your perfumes,
O heavenly Spouse!
I will run and not tire,
> *until You bring me into the wine-cellar,*
> *until Your left hand is under my head*
> *and Your right hand will embrace me happily*
> *[and] You will kiss me with the happiest*
kiss of Your mouth.

— Saint Clare of Assisi

Nearly 400 years before Teresa and John of the Cross gave us their love songs in Spanish, Clare and Francis of Assisi were causing a love revolution in 13th-century Italy. They were both ecstatics, and in this poem Clare sings of her love of God as if He were a classic Italian lover—all fragrance, wine, and kisses. Some will say that human love is a pale reflection of the experience of union with God, but it is surely the closest metaphor we can find—which is why it has been used in all traditions throughout time. As Clare would have known, the prototypical love poem in the Judeo-Christian tradition is the Song of Solomon, which begins with these lines:

Let him kiss me with the kisses of his mouth: for thy love is
*   better than wine.*
Because of the savor of thy good ointments thy name is as
ointment poured forth, therefore do the virgins love thee.

———◆———

Thirst

*Another morning and I wake with thirst
for the goodness I do not have. I walk
out to the pond and all the way God has
given us such beautiful lessons. Oh Lord,
I was never a quick scholar but sulked
and hunched over my books past the
hour and the bell; grant me, in your
mercy, a little more time. Love for the
earth and love for you are having such a
long conversation in my heart. Who
knows what will finally happen or
where I will be sent, yet already I have
given a great many things away, expect-
ing to be told to pack nothing, except the
prayers which, with this thirst, I am
slowly learning.*

— Mary Oliver

Mary Oliver's luminous, lyrical poems are among the most well known and loved in America. For much of her life, her church has been Nature. Of all contemporary American poets, hers is the voice that most celebrates and praises the natural world in terms of reverence.

Since her life partner, Molly Malone Cook, died in 2005, her work has become more explicitly Christian, while still praising in the Church of Nature. What especially moves me in this beautiful poem is how the longing to be made "good"—not as in *being* good, I would suggest, but as in being made authentic—is the inspiration, the fountainhead, of her prayers.

———◆———

I am, you anxious one

I am, you anxious one.

Don't you sense me, ready to break
into being at your touch?
My murmurings surround you like shadowy wings.
Can't you see me standing before you
cloaked in stillness?
Hasn't my longing ripened in you
from the beginning
as fruit ripens on a branch?

I am the dream you are dreaming.
When you want to awaken, I am that wanting:
I grow strong in the beauty you behold.
And with the silence of stars I enfold
your cities made by time.

— Rainer Maria Rilke

How can we expect not to be anxious, Rilke implies, if we do not feel a greater presence, cloaked in stillness, with us in our days? Yet that same anxiety is the fuel for our longing, itself a sign of the presence we thirst for. Rilke was not a conventional Christian by any means, but his life was marked by a constant search for the authentic ground of his native religion.

His work is shot through and through with an original spiritual sensibility that was shaped in large part by the Christian culture of central Europe that he grew up in. This poem is one of 67 that comprise The Book of Monastic Life, which he wrote in 25 days in the persona of a Russian monk. Rilke had recently returned from a visit to Russia and had been profoundly moved by the instinctual and passionate expression of religious feeling that he witnessed there.

———◆———

Walk in the Dark

If a man
wishes to be sure
of the road he travels on,
he must close his eyes
and walk in the dark.

— *Saint John of the Cross*

So the less we know, the more sure we may be? John of the Cross frequently turns conventional wisdom on its head, and nowhere more so than here. The light of the left brain will not serve us on the mystical path. When our thoughts no longer fill the screen of our awareness, we are in a state of unknowing, because we normally "know" through our thinking. But when thinking falls away and we enter the apparent darkness of not thinking, we discover another kind of knowing, another kind of light. Wordless, imageless—it is the essence of silence itself, and it carries its own knowledge, which is faith, our true guide. Faith, not belief, carries us forward; for a belief is a thought, whereas faith is a knowing, a certainty which grows in the marrow.

———◆———

Daydreaming

I believe that the root of evil,
in everybody perhaps,
but certainly in those whom
affliction has touched,
is daydreaming.
It is the sole consolation,
the unique resource of the afflicted;
the one solace that helps them bear
the fearful burden of time;
and a very innocent one,
besides being indispensable.
So how could it be possible to renounce it?
It has only one disadvantage,
which is that it is unreal.
To renounce it for the love of truth
is really to abandon all one's possessions
in a mad excess of love and to follow Him
who is the personification of Truth.
And it is really to bear the cross;
because time is the cross.
In all its forms without exception,
daydreaming is falsehood.
It excludes love. Love is real.

— Simone Weil

Simone Weil's faith and life were rigorous and exacting, and these words carry that same keen blade. Daydreaming is the act of not being present to where one is, no matter how consoling it may be as an activity—especially for those whose present experience is painful. Daydreaming is a denial of love. Love requires our presence and our fullness, our embrace of life as it is showing up in the moment, however painful it may be. Simone Weil, who ended up dying of starvation in solidarity with French soldiers who were not getting enough rations in World War II, put her life on the line for principles like these. Daydreaming—not the activity of having thoughts, but allowing one's attention to get lost in them—is seen as an obstacle to contemplative practices in all traditions.

———◆———

The Sum of Perfection

Creation forgotten,
Creator only known,
Attention turned inward
In love with the Beloved alone.

— *Saint John of the Cross*

Love for John of the Cross is an interior condition of union, with no external object of reference in either the world or in the mind. All attachment to the things and thoughts of this world has fallen away. Imageless, wordless, there is nothing to say, nowhere to go and nothing to do when such a blessedness descends. This poem has all the brevity, clarity, and completeness of a Japanese haiku (though not the exact form of seventeen syllables in three lines) used by Zen practitioner-poets on the other side of the world to deliver their own pithy wisdom. Its chant-like quality is more apparent in the original Spanish:

Olvido de lo criado,
memoria del Criador,
atención a lo interior
y estarse amando al Amado.

———◆———

Love (excerpt)

If I speak in the tongues of men and angels,
but have not love,
I am only a resounding gong or a clanging cymbal.
And if I have the gift of prophecy
and can fathom all mysteries and all knowledge,
and if I have a faith that can move mountains,
but have not love, I am nothing.
And if I give all I possess to the poor and
surrender my body to the flames,
but have not love, I gain nothing.
. . . .
When I was a child,
I talked like a child,
I thought like a child,
I reasoned like a child.
When I became [an adult],
I put childish ways behind me.
Now we see but a poor reflection as in a mirror; then we shall see
face to face.
Now I know in part; then I shall know fully, even as I am fully
known.
And now these three remain:
faith, hope and love.
But the greatest of these is love.

— *Saint Paul, 1 Corinthians 13:1–3, 11–13*

Paul's letters, written between A.D. 50 and 60, are the earliest part of the New Testament. He is sometimes called the first Christian mystic, and he is known to have had, not only the famous visionary conversion experience on the road to Damascus but also an ineffable rapture referred to in 2 Corinthians 12:2–4. He was also known in his time for the gift of tongues, and prophetic visions. So his experience of Christ was received not from external sources but from direct inner revelation. In this inspired letter he affirms that good works, visions, and ecstatic experiences of any kind are of no value if we "have not love." Love, not spiritual gifts and powers, is the central message of Christ.

———◆———

The divine will

The divine will
is a deep abyss
of which the present
moment is the entrance.
If you plunge
into this abyss
you will find it
infinitely more vast
than your
desires.

— *Jean Pierre de Caussade*

Way back in the early 18th century, long before Eckhart Tolle's *The Power of Now* became a global bestseller, the French Jesuit Jean Pierre de Caussade coined the memorable phrase "the sacrament of the present moment." "It is necessary," he said, "to be disengaged from all we feel and do in order to walk with God in the duty of the present moment . . . We must confine ourselves to the present moment without taking thought for the one before or the one to come." Yet the present moment is not so much what is happening now (although attention to what is happening can be an avenue to it) as it is the context, the field, within what is happening takes place. It is the silent, spacious presence that is the root and ground of all that happens. If you want to know God's will, de Caussade says in these few brilliant lines, become that presence.

———◆———

The Inferno (excerpt)

Midway on our life's journey, I found myself
In dark woods, the right road lost. To tell
About those woods is hard—so tangled and rough

And savage that thinking of it now, I feel
The old fear stirring: death is hardly more bitter.
And yet, to treat the good I found there as well

I'll tell what I saw, though how I came to enter
I cannot well say, being so full of sleep
Whatever moment it was I began to blunder

Off the true path. But when I came to stop
Below a hill that marked one end of the valley
That had pierced my heart with terror, I looked up

Toward the crest and saw its shoulders already
Mantled in rays of that bright planet that shows
The road to everyone, whatever our journey.

Then I could feel the terror begin to ease
That churned in my heart's lake all through the night.
— Dante Alighieri

Dante's great work, *The Divine Comedy*, charts the soul's trials and eventual ascent to God in a story that is a cornerstone of European literature and culture. From Homer on, the soul's journey has been a quintessentially Western and also Christian theme. We live in time as well as in eternity. We value history and evolution as well as the timeless Now. We all know periods like the one described in this, the most famous passage in Dante's entire work, of feeling lost in a dark wood, having wandered away from the right path. But if we did not stray, there would be no story and no journey.

As the Sufi poet Rumi, who lived in the same century as Dante, says, *straying maps the path*. The straying, the falling asleep, seems to lead us away from our goal, but in fact it is only being lost that allows us to be found; we only wake up when we have been asleep. There, at his lowest ebb, when he acknowledges how lost he feels, something in him prompts Dante to look up—to look up from his self pity and self absorption. He raises his head and sees the dawn, the sun rising over a mountain, perennial symbol of the light of consciousness as well as of Christ. His heart is put at ease, and he continues on his way, ready to meet what comes.

———◆———

✒ Canticle to the Waterbirds (excerpt)

Clack your beaks you cormorants and kittiwakes,
North on those rock-croppings finger-jutted
into the rough Pacific surge;
You migratory terns and pipers who leave
but the temporal clawtrack written on
sandbars there of your presence;
Grebes and pelicans; you comber-picking
scoters and you shorelong gulls;
All you keepers of the coastline
* north of here to the Mendocino beaches;*
All you beyond upon the cliff-face
* thwarting the surf at Hecate Head;*
Hovering the under-surge where
the cold Columbia grapples at the bar;
North yet to the Sound, whose islands
float like a sown flurry of chips
upon the sea: Break wide your harsh and salt-encrusted beaks
unmade for song,
And say a praise up to the Lord.
. . . .

But may you, birds,
utterly seized in God's supremacy,
Austerely living under His austere eye—
Yet may you teach a man a necessary thing to know,
Which has to do of the strict conformity that creaturehood entails,
And constitutes the prime commitment all things share.
For God has given you the imponderable grace to be this
verification, Outside the mulled incertitude of our forensic choices;
That you, our lesser in the rich hegemony of Being,
May serve as testament to what a creature is,
And what creation owes.

Curlews, stilts and scissortails, beachcomber gulls.
Wave-haunters, shore-keepers, rockhead-holders, all cape-top
vigilantes,
Now give God praise.
Send up the strict articulation of your throats,
And say His name.

— *Brother Antoninus (William Everson)*

34

William Everson's birds float through this magnificent poem as the harbingers of wisdom. Everson wrote it while he was working in a soup kitchen in Oakland in 1950, just before he joined the Dominican Order and took the name of Brother Antoninus. The wisdom of the birds lies in their complete absorption in the present moment and in their unquestioning obedience to the will of God, which amounts to the same thing. Echoing Dante and also Saint Francis, Everson suggests that the birds are closer to God precisely because they are lower on the scale of free will and self consciousness than human beings—they are *our lesser in the rich hegemony of Being,* and yet this is why they

May serve as testament to what a creature is
And what Creation owes.

Everything they do is in accordance with Divine Will—*utterly seized in God's supremacy*—so everything they do is praise. What Creation owes is praise, and the birds, representing all creatures lower on the evolutionary scale than us, show us the way. And Everson names them in their particular uniqueness, making clear that every single aspect of Creation matters; each has its own dignity and place. In gathering up the whole circle of life and calling it sacred, the poem is a resounding riposte to those who act as if human reason would have us stand above and separate from the rest of all living things.

———◆———

Unholy Sonnet 4

Amazing to believe that nothingness
Surrounds us with delight and lets us be,
And that the meekness of nonentity,
Despite the friction of the world of sense,
Despite the leveling of violence,
Is all that matters. All the energy
We force into the matchhead and the city
Explodes inside a loving emptiness.

Not Dante's rings, not the Zen zero's mouth,
Out of which comes and into which light goes,
This God recedes from every metaphor,
Turns the hardest data into untruth,
And fills all blanks with blankness. This love shows
Itself in absence, which the stars adore.

— *Mark Jarman*

This poem presents a profoundly countercultural message: *the meekness of nonentity . . . is all that matters.* The prevailing wisdom of American culture is that the individual should aspire to be special, to stand out from the crowd. Jarman, on the other hand, is saying here that what matters is to disappear. But to disappear from what? From our identification with the ego, which always wants to feel special. When we are in the silent ground, in what he calls the *nothingness,* we are truly ourselves, one with everything, and in that sense, absent as a separate ego. Jarman is a contemporary Christian, and while he echoes here the long *via negativa* tradition begun by Dionysius the Areopagite in the 6th century, he also echoes the Zen tradition, in which the practitioner aspires to become "a man of no rank." And yet no metaphors of any tradition, East or West, can come close to the reality of that love which *shows itself in absence.*

———◆———

First Love (excerpt)

It was a flower.
. . . .
suddenly
there was Before I saw it, the vague
past, and Now. Forever. Nearby
was the sandy sweep of the Roman Road,
and where we sat the grass was thin.
From a bare patch of that poor soil, solitary,
sprang the flower, face upturned,
looking completely, openly into my eyes.
I was barely old enough to ask
and repeat its name.

'Convulvulus,' said my mother.
Pale shell-pink, a chalice
no wider across than a silver sixpence.

It looked at me, I looked back,
delight filled me as if
I, not the flower,
were a flower and were brimful of rain.
And there was endlessness.
Perhaps through a lifetime what I've desired
has always been to return
to that endless giving and receiving,
the wholeness of that attention,
that once-in-a-lifetime
secret communion.

— Denise Levertov

This is one of the more beautiful illustrations of a moment captured in language. It is not an accident, I believe, that Levertov was a young child when she felt the boundaries dissolve between herself and a flower to reveal the *endlessness*. As children the veil between ourselves and the world is thinner than when we are adults. Levertov was the daughter of an English minister, and her inner experience as a Christian, as distinct to the outer forms of Church dogma and belief, informs much of her work. The true communion, she tells us in this poem, available in every moment, and in every moment unique (*once-in-a-lifetime*) is

that endless giving and receiving, the wholeness
of that attention.

———◆———

For the Time Being: Xmas Oratorio (excerpt)

1V

Chorus

He is the Way.
Follow Him through the Land of Unlikeness;
You will see rare beasts, and have unique adventures.

He is the Truth.
Seek Him in the Kingdom of Anxiety;
You will come to a great city that has expected your return for
years.

He is the Life.
Love Him in the world of the Flesh;
And at your marriage all its occasions shall dance for joy.

— W.H. Auden

Auden's famous poem "For The Time Being: Xmas Oratorio" was written on the heels of his conversion to the Anglican faith. This, the poem's last section, overturns conventional wisdom and would have us seek God—not in some holy, uplifting experience nor in church sacraments and ritual—but in the confusing and uncertain world we live in from day to day. Earlier in this long poem, Auden uses his gift for comic imagery to suggest that we are less likely to experience any sense of redemption over Xmas, with all its glitter and gifts, so much as in the drab period of the year that follows. There, where we would never imagine Him to be, seek Him: in the land of *Unlikeness, the Kingdom of Anxiety,* and in the *world of the Flesh,* seek Him.

Unlikeness: How difficult it can be to see ourselves in the opposite party, the "enemy," the ugly, the cruel, or the violent. How can the Kingdom of Heaven, of Peace, exist within our anxieties? And yet, the poet says, that city is ever present and patiently awaits our return. And above all, perhaps, seek Him not in some other sphere, nor expect all to be well after death, but seek Him right here and now in this complicated and messy world of the flesh and the appetites.

———◆———

Love (III)

Love bade me welcome: yet my soul drew back,
        Guilty of dust and sin.
But quick-eyed Love, observing me grow slack
        From my first entrance in,
Drew nearer to me, sweetly questioning
        If I lacked anything.

"A guest," I answered, "worthy to be here":
        Love said, "You shall be he."
"I, the unkind, ungrateful? Ah, my dear,
        I cannot look on Thee."
Love took my hand, and smiling did reply,
        "Who made the eyes but I?"

"Truth Lord, but I have marred them: let my shame
        Go where it doth deserve."
"And know you not," says Love, "who bore the blame?"
        "My dear, then I will serve."
"You must sit down," says Love, "and taste my meat."
        So I did sit and eat.

— George Herbert

More than a few of us, given the popularity of this poem over 400 years, tend to draw back at the prospect of unconditional love, feeling overwhelmed and unworthy of it. Yet no matter how undeserving we feel, the Christian message is that we are already loved completely. George Herbert, a 17th-century English Protestant, captures this beautifully in his famous poem. No effort on our part, either through good works or sustained spiritual endeavors, can substitute for the sheer grace that is always and ever available to us. All (!) that is required is an acknowledgment of our own divisions and failings. Herbert's poem—which inspired Simone Weil, the French mystic whose words can be found in this collection, to become a Christian—adopts the conversational style of not only lovers but also friends, and the intimacy of friendship with God has been one of the many themes that has traced its way all through the Christian tradition.

———◆———

November 1938 (excerpt)

If only I could enter
the sanctuary of the poem,
naked as a spirit,

my miserable flesh
shed in a heap on the porch—
like at Easter in Solesmes,

when the plain song
plucked me aloft
from my suffering

and I hovered like a feather
on the breath of God,
or dust in his splendor,

far above the malheur, dégoût et
paresse of my unworthy life:
Love bade me welcome, Love.

— *Paula Tatarunis*

Paula Tatarunis, an East Coast M.D. who also happens to be a superb poet, wrote this as a response to George Herbert's poem "Love (III)." The moment love bade her welcome occurred in the Abbey of Solesmes in France, which is well known for its revival of Gregorian chant, or plainsong. The *malheur, dégoût et. paresse*—the suffering, disgust, and laziness—of her life was left behind in the soaring of her soul on the waves of the plainsong.

———◆———

God is a pure no-thing

God is a pure no-thing,
    concealed in now and here:
the less you reach for him,
    the more he will appear.

— *Angelus Silesius*

God is a pure no-thing—what a power there is in this first line—the power to break open the mind, to shatter whatever concepts and images we may have of the Divine, and to fill us with the living mystery of the only thing we can know for certain—the palpable presence of the here and now. Angelus Silesius was a Catholic and fierce advocate of the Counter-Reformation who lived in 17th-century Germany. Silesius is a clarion voice in the Christian *via negativa* tradition. He tells us here that seeking is not the way to find God; rather, in our open embrace of what is before us in the present moment, He may reveal Himself—not as a form, or thought, or even as a feeling, but as an ungraspable, unnamable *no-thing*.

———◆———

One thing alone I crave (excerpt)

One thing alone I crave
namely
All in everything

This One
I seek
the only One
do I desire
. . . .
What or Who this One is
I may not say
can never feel
Nothing
more or less
is there to say

For the One is not simply in all
the One Being is over all

YOU are my GOD
holding me
within my very SELF

— Dame Catherine Gascoigne

In this poem Dame Catherine asserts that she not only has no words for Who this One is that she craves; there is no feeling that can express it either. It is not enough to say the One is in all, which would be pantheism; rather, this One is both Creation and beyond it at the same time, irreducible to any name or concept at all. Like Angelus Silesius, Dame Catherine lived in the 17th century. She was an English Catholic who fled the Protestant and Puritan government in England and became abbess of the monastery of Cambrai in Belgium. There she became at odds with the Catholic hierarchy for not teaching the then fashionable spiritual exercises of the Jesuits. Instead, her contemplative practice followed the example of earlier English mystics like Julian of Norwich and the anonymous author of *The Cloud of Unknowing*, who emphasized silence rather than visualizations and spoken prayer.

———◆———

We awaken in Christ's body

We awaken in Christ's body
as Christ awakens our bodies,
and my poor hand is Christ, He enters
my foot, and is infinitely me.

I move my hand, and wonderfully
my hand becomes Christ, becomes all of Him
(for God is indivisibly
whole, seamless in His Godhood).

I move my foot, and at once
He appears like a flash of lightning.
Do my words seem blasphemous?—Then
open your heart to Him

and let yourself receive the one
who is opening to you so deeply.
For if we genuinely love Him,
we wake up inside Christ's body

where all our body, all over,
every most hidden part of it,
is realized in joy as Him,
and He makes us, utterly, real,

and everything that is hurt, everything
that seemed to us dark, harsh, shameful,
maimed, ugly, irreparably
damaged, is in Him transformed

and recognized as whole, as lovely,
and radiant in His light
we awaken as the Beloved
in every last part of our body.

— Saint Symeon the New Theologian

We awaken in Christ's body
as Christ awakens our bodies,

Symeon's awakening, or realization, takes place not in the mind, not even in the heart alone, but throughout the entire physical being. This seems to me the most beautiful affirmation of the physical world, so unusual in the more canonical Christian texts and yet so resonant with the Christian promise of broken bodies being made whole, of the transfiguration of Christ. Except the transfiguration that Symeon speaks of takes place, not in the historical time of Jesus, nor on some future Judgment Day, but here and now for any individual who is able to *genuinely love Him*, by which Symeon means to forget oneself and disappear in that love. To become zero. In these lines, Symeon dissolves the schism between body and spirit, mind and heart, this world and any other.

Saint Symeon, a 10th-century monastic in Byzantium, continues to inspire Orthodox Christians today through his writings in the *Philokalia*, the collection of wisdom teachings by the early Desert Fathers.

———◆———

You Are Christ's Hands

Christ has no body now on earth but yours,
no hands but yours,
no feet but yours,
Yours are the eyes through which is to look out
Christ's compassion to the world
Yours are the feet with which he is to go about
doing good;
Yours are the hands with which he is to bless men now.

— Saint Teresa of Ávila

Some six centuries later, Saint Teresa's words echo those of Saint Symeon yet with a different emphasis. She was not only a mystic but also an active member of society. She was a product of the Western Church which, in contrast to the Orthodox tradition, advocates good works in the world as an expression of faith. The accent in this poem is less on the inner awakening itself—though that is implied—than on its usefulness in service to others and perhaps to the Church itself. Your hands are Christ's hands, and they have work to do.

———◆———

The Pentecost Castle, 15 (excerpt)

I shall go down
to the lovers' well
and wash this wound
that will not heal

beloved soul
what shall you see
nothing at all
yet eye to eye

depths of non-being
perhaps too clear
my desire dying
as I desire

— *Geoffrey Hill*

The first verse of this, the last section of Hill's long poem, "Pentecost Castle," strikes me like an arrow. Geoffrey Hill, whose writing is infused with his Anglican faith, is one of Britain's best-known contemporary poets. Here, he hits the mark; the truth that our wounds, not our talents and gifts, open the door to Christ and His healing balm of the Holy Spirit. The French word for "wound," *blessure*, has the same root as *blessing*. The silence of contemplative practice is not intended to smooth over our pains; on the contrary, it draws them up from deep down in our own well, and they are our offering to Christ, whose wounds join us to Him. When we wash in the lover's well the silence lays bare the wound and brings us *eye to eye* with what seems to the senses to be *nothing at all*. Yet that nothing, we discover, is itself the healing balm—a spacious and overflowing fullness, which in an earlier section of the same poem, Hill calls an *emptiness ever thronging*.

———◆———

Little Gidding (excerpt)

The dove descending breaks the air
With flame of incandescent terror
Of which the tongues declare
The one discharge from sin and error.
The only hope, or else despair
  Lies in the choice of pyre or pyre—
  To be redeemed from fire by fire.

Who then devised the torment? Love.
Love is the unfamiliar Name
Behind the hands that wove
The intolerable shirt of flame
Which human power cannot remove.
  We only live, only suspire,
  Consumed by either fire or fire.

— T.S. Eliot

Eliot's great poem "The Four Quartets," one of the finest works of 20th-century literature, offers plenty of challenges as well as inspiration to its readers. Densely layered throughout with literary and religious allusions, it also contains frequent though obscure references to the time and place in which it appeared, Britain in the Second World War. "Little Gidding," the name of the fourth quartet, is a hamlet in the English countryside where the first Anglican lay community was founded in 1625. Eliot visited the surviving church in 1936 and had an epiphany that inspired him to write this, the last of his quartets.

The way time intersects with the timeless is a theme that weaves its way throughout the work. The images of dove and fire allude both to the Battle of Britain and the Holy Spirit. The "dark" dove is the enemy bomber, carrier of death, the incendiary bomb with its *flame of incandescent terror.* The bomb's flickering tongues of fire make it a kind of serpent, and its fires become the fires of Hell. The "light" dove is the Pentecostal fire, the fire of inspiration and purification. The whole dilemma of man is bound up in his capacity for choice—the choice between these two fires.

———◆———

Santa Teresa's Book-Mark

Let nothing disturb thee,
Nothing affright thee;
All things are passing;
God never changeth;
Patient endurance
Attaineth to all things;
Who God possesseth
In nothing is wanting;
Alone God sufficeth.

— *Saint Teresa of Ávila*

There is a deep calm and acceptance of life as it is in these words of Saint Teresa. To accept deeply that all things are passing is to allow life to sound its changes as it must, without clinging to some anchor in the temporal world, whether it be our looks, a relationship, work, or position in the world. The only anchor that holds firm is what is beyond time and place, in that which never changes. There lies our contentment and our fulfillment.

———◆———

The madness of love

The madness of love
Is a blessed fate;
And if we understood this
We would seek no other:
It brings into unity
What was divided,
And this is the truth:
Bitterness it makes sweet,
It makes the stranger a neighbor,
And what was lowly it raises on high.

— Hadewijch of Antwerp

Love is a madness, but a madness which is the greatest of all blessings. Love turns everything upside down; what is sane becomes mad, and what is mad becomes sane. The lover may dance and sing for no reason, or sit in a corner in silence for hours. But whatever she does, her world is whole.

It brings into unity
What was divided,

Hadewijch, like her 13th-century contemporary, Saint Francis, was a fool for God. Except Hadewijch never had the formality of a religious order within which to express her love. She was a lay practitioner in Belgium, of high birth and well educated, who traveled extensively. She was associated with the Beguines, lay communities of women who took no vows and who were often suspected of heresy.

———◆———

All things

All things
are too small
to hold me,
I am so vast

In the Infinite
I reach
for the Uncreated

I have
touched it,
it undoes me
wider than wide

Everything else
is too narrow

You know this well,
you who are also there

— Hadewijch II

Hadewijch II, about whom almost nothing is known, also lived in the 13th century. The 16 poems of hers that survive, written in couplets, have a markedly different tone than the work of Hadewijch of Antwerp. Her work is more metaphysical, more intellectual, than that of her namesake, for whom love was the royal way. In this wonderful poem her consciousness seems to have become one with the universe. In touching the Uncreated, which is prior to all form, she herself is undone, meaning she too has fallen beyond any concept of her own form or identity, which will always be too narrow to contain the Infinite she now is.

———◆———

Tighten

Tighten
to nothing
the circle
that is
the world's things.

Then the Naked
circle
can grow wide,
enlarging,
embracing all

— Hadewijch II

The simplicity and rigor of these lines take my breath away with every reading. I imagine a noose being drawn around everything that makes up my worldly concerns, tighter and tighter until nothing remains. Then, having disappeared into zero, like a black hole, the noose turns back out on itself and spreads its luminous nakedness, its no-thingness, out over all that is.

———◆———

The Love of Truth

*to face affliction . . . a man must be prepared, for the
love of truth, to accept the death of the soul.*

. . . .

*It is
impossible to accept that death of the soul unless
one possesses another life, outside of the soul's
illusory life . . . outside all one's thoughts and
feelings and outside everything knowable, in the
hands of our Father who is in secret. Of those who
have done this, one can say that they have been born
of water and Spirit; for they are no longer anything
but a twofold obedience—on the one side to the
mechanical necessity in which their earthly condition
involves them, and on the other to the divine
inspiration. There is nothing left in them which one
could call their own will, their person, their 'I'. They
have become nothing other than a certain intersection
of nature and God.*

— Simone Weil

It's all or nothing for Simone Weil. By the death of the soul she means the death of the personal self—the complex of thoughts and feelings that make up our familiar identity. What is striking in this passage is her assertion that when this happens, a person is subject not just to divine will but also to mechanical necessity, with the implication that the world of causes and conditions has its own laws that operate automatically, outside the sphere of influence of God's will (except perhaps for the incursion of grace). The implication is that just because the personal self has fallen away, it does not mean there will be no more suffering. Suffering is in the nature of nature. Essentially, it is not personal.

———◆———

I Came to Love You Too Late

I came to love you too late, Oh Beauty,
so ancient and so new. Yes,
I came to love you too late. What did I know?
You were inside me, and I was
out of my body and mind looking
for you.
I drove like an ugly madman against
the beautiful things and beings
you made.
You were inside me, but I was not inside you....
You called to me, you cried to me; you broke the bowl
of my deafness; you uncovered my beams and threw them
at me; you rejected my blindness; you blew a fragrant wind
on me, and
I sucked in my breath and wanted you; I tasted you
and now I want you as I want food and water; you
touched me, and I have been burning ever since to
have your peace.

— Saint Augustine

Such searing lines of longing Saint Augustine writes here—such a poignant description of the self-willed individual, the one who wants to take life by storm, only to fall at last to his knees and see that what he has been seeking has been there all along. He finally realizes that the Beauty he seeks is not outside but has been inside him all along. Augustine's use of the term *Beauty* points to the deep influence on him of neo-Platonic thought, which was so prevalent in the early Church. It might seem ironic that Augustine, who railed so vehemently against the inherent sinfulness of the body, should use such erotic terms in passages like this to describe the longing of the lover for the beloved. But then he had a deeply passionate nature, and while he led something of a dissolute youth, the same forces of desire were turned in another direction in his religious life.

———◆———

For the Asking

You would not seek Me if you did not already possess Me. — Pascal

Augustine said his soul
was a house so cramped
God could barely squeeze in.
Knock down the mean partitions,
he prayed, so You may enter!
Raise the oppressive ceilings!
                    Augustine's soul
didn't become a mansion large enough
to welcome, along with God, the women he'd loved,
except for his mother (though one, perhaps,
his son's mother, did remain to inhabit
a small dark room). God, therefore,
would never have felt
fully at home as his guest.
                    Nevertheless,
it's clear desire
fulfilled itself in the asking, revealing prayer's
dynamic action, that scoops out channels
like water on stone, or builds like layers
of grainy sediment steadily
forming sandstone. The walls, with each thought,
each feeling, each word he set down,
expanded, unnoticed; the roof
rose, and a skylight opened.

— Denise Levertov

Levertov's riff on Augustine's "I Came To Love You Too Late" is consoling; for all Augustine's angst, chest beating, and searing longing, he is already found. The *dynamic action* of prayer, the intensity of the asking itself, lights up synapses in the brain, plows a neurobiological furrow along which the response can stream. To love God is no abstract matter; its proof lies in the love you offer into your life. Augustine somehow forgot to love the women he had known, which is why God could never have felt

fully at home as his guest.

Yet we are all imperfect in our loving, and the intensity of Augustine's longing was such that

the roof
rose, and a skylight opened.

—————◆—————

You who want

You who want
knowledge,
seek the Oneness
within

There you
will find
the clear mirror
already waiting

— Hadewijch II

Hadewijch says much the same as Augustine in these lines, but in far cooler and more measured terms. Her use of the mirror image echoes the "empty mirror" metaphor used in Zen. The mirror is empty because the one who was looking has fallen away, leaving no reflection.

Hadewijch II wrote this in 13th-century Europe when knowledge was not something that a Christian would be expected to look for. All the knowledge you needed would be given to you by your priest, who would dispense to you his understanding of the teachings of the Church. Even reading the Bible on your own was not encouraged; after all, you might form opinions of your own. Questions were not welcome or customary. Yet within this strict and rigid religious atmosphere, there were always some, like Hadewijch II, who knew that true knowledge lies within.

———◆———

Wring Out My Clothes

*Such love does
the sky now pour,
that whenever I stand in a field,*

*I have to wring out the light
when I get
home.*

— Saint Francis of Assisi

Saint Francis is a fool for God—I can just imagine him doing this—wringing out the light from his clothes after a day in the Umbrian countryside. He is ecstatic with the downpouring of love he feels from his Creator. For light is love and wisdom made visible, and he is drenched in it. This is another Daniel Ladinsky rendering, and it shows, both in the simplicity and in the surprising humor of a single image. It is entirely in the mood and tone of Saint Francis, who would spend as much time in nature as in any church.

———◆———

Granum Sinapis (excerpt)

Become as a child,
become deaf, become blind!
Your own substance
must become nothingness;
drive all substance, all nothingness far from you!
Leave space, leave time,
eschew also all physical representation.
Go without a way
the narrow foot-path,
then you will succeed in finding the desert.

O my soul,
go out, let God in!
Sink, my entire being,
into God's nothingness,
sink into the bottomless flood!
If I flee from you,
you come to me,
if I lose myself,
I find you:
O goodness extending over all being.

— Anonymous

When the writer of "Granum Sinapis" speaks of becoming nothingness, it suggests to me that we need do nothing by our own will, that we have only to let go of all striving and effort and open ourselves to the deep waters of existence. Without technique, without trying to seek anything, being only awake and attentive to the moment, we may enter *the desert*, the luminous ground of silence. "Granum Sinapis," the Latin for a grain of mustard seed, was probably written in Germany sometime in the 14th century. It carries the flavor of Meister Eckhart and may have been written by one of his students—or even by the master himself.

———◆———

One Must Go Beyond God

Where is my dwelling place? Where I can never stand.
Where is my final goal, toward which I should ascend?
It is beyond all place. What should my quest then be?
I must, transcending God, into the desert flee.

— Angelus Silesius

The desert again, this time from Angelus Silesius. It is an image that has been used by Christians from the Desert Fathers of the 3rd and 4th centuries, right down to Thomas Merton, who wrote in the mid-20th century that the prayer of the desert was the deepest prayer of all. The desert is beyond all our notions of God or anything else. It is beyond time and place, beyond all description. It is the most solid ground and at the same time no ground at all.

———◆———

Without a Place and With a Place

Without a place and with a place
to rest—living darkly with no ray
of light—I burn my self away.

My soul—no longer bound—is free
from the creations of the world;
above itself it rises hurled
into a life of ecstasy,
leaning only on God. The world
will therefore clarify at last
what I esteem of highest grace:
my soul revealing it can rest
without a place and with a place.

Although I suffer a dark night
in mortal life, I also know
my agony is slight, for though
I am in darkness without light,
a clear heavenly life I know;
for love gives power to my life,
however black and blind my day,
to yield my soul, and free of strife
to rest—living darkly with no ray.

Love can perform a wondrous labor
which I have learned internally,
and all the good or bad in me
takes on a penetrating savor,
changing my soul so it can be
consumed in a delicious flame.
I feel it in me as a ray;
and quickly killing every trace
of light—I burn my self away.

— *Saint John of the Cross*

This beautiful poem by Saint John of the Cross adds some further texture and depth to the themes of the previous few poems. Everything in his personality—the good and the bad—is fuel for the fire that burns inside his breast. His body and being are an alchemical retort to which the flame of love is applied. Gradually, everything he knows himself to be is burned away in love's flame, *killing every trace of light.* In the darkness that remains, a light can burn that is never seen by mortal eyes.

———◆———

The Mystical Theology (excerpt)

Guide of Christians
in the wisdom of heaven!
Lead us up beyond unknowing and light,
up to the farthest, highest peak
of mystic scripture,
where the mysteries of God's Word
lie simple, absolute, and unchangeable
in the brilliant darkness of a hidden silence.
Amid the deepest shadow
they pour overwhelming light
on what is most manifest.
Amid the wholly unsensed and unseen
they completely fill our sightless minds
with treasures beyond all beauty.

— Dionysius the Areopagite

The rapture of this poem could be that of a lover, and it is, except this lover is in love with a beloved who has no name or form. His mind is *sightless* yet filled with the treasures of God's mysteries, which are beyond all earthly notions of beauty. Not much is known about the author of the works written under the pseudonym of Dionysius the Areopagite, who was a convert of Saint Paul's mentioned in Acts. But he is generally considered to have been a scholar living in the early 6th century and to have possibly come from Syria. Also known as Pseudo-Dionysius, his work shows a profound knowledge and appreciation for the neo-Platonists, as well as of the Old and New Testaments.

———◆———

Adventures in New Testament Greek: Nous (excerpt)

When even the handy lexicon cannot
quite place the nous as anything beyond
one rustic ancestor of reason, you might

be satisfied to trouble the odd term
no further—and so would fail to find
your way to it, most fruitful faculty

untried. Dormant in its roaring cave,
the heart's intellective aptitude grows dim,
unless you find a way to wake it. So,

let's try something, even now. Even as
you tend these lines, attend for a moment
to your breath as you draw it in: regard

the breath's cool descent, a stream from mouth
to throat to the furnace of the heart.
Observe that queer, cool confluence of breath

and blood, and do your thinking there.

— Scott Cairns

Nous is the Greek term for the intelligence of the heart, what some traditions call the heart-mind. This poem Scott Cairns, a contemporary Orthodox Christian, places it at the center of the ancient Orthodox practice known as the prayer of the heart, or the Jesus prayer. The contemplative follows the breath down into the chest, mentally carrying with it the name of Jesus, or another sacred word, such as Abba. The Sufis of Islam follow the same practice with their own sacred words, as do the Hindus with their mantras. The prayer of the heart was widely practiced among the Desert Fathers in the early centuries after Christ and is described in detail in the Philokalia, the collection of their writings. Its purpose is to join the mind with the body in the heart and to make accessible the knowledge that only the heart can know.

———◆———

Beguines say I err . . .

O my Lover, what will beguines say
and religious types,
When they hear the excellence
of your divine song?
Beguines say I err,
priests, clerics, and Preachers
Augustinians, Carmelites,
and the Friars Minor,
Because I wrote about the being
of the one purified by Love.
I do not make Reason safe for them,
who makes them say this to me...

I have said that I will love Him.
I lie, for I am not.
It is He alone who loves me:
He is, and I am not;
And nothing more is necessary to me
Than what He wills,
And that He is worthy.
He is fullness,
And by this I am impregnated,
This is the divine seed and Loyal Love.

— Marguerite Porete

Marguerite Porete would be a radical woman's voice in any age, but in the 13th century her words must have been incendiary. She referred to the established Church as the "Little Holy Church" and contrasted it to the "Great Holy Church," meaning those enlightened souls who had lost themselves in God. Even the Beguines were likely to be offended by her writings, she says in this poem because she so clearly challenges dogma and reason. She has been impregnated by the Divine seed, and in that holy love-making, she herself has disappeared, leaving only her Lord living and breathing through her body and mind.

———◆———

On Prayer (excerpt)

Then a priestess said, Speak to us of Prayer.
And he answered, saying:
You pray in your distress and in your need; would that you might pray
    also in the fullness of your joy and in your days of abundance

. . . .

It is enough that you enter the temple invisible
I cannot teach you how to pray in words.
God listens not to your words save when He Himself utters them
    through your lips.
And I cannot teach you the prayer of the seas and the forests and the
mountains.
But you who are born of the mountains and the forests and the seas
    can find their prayer in your heart,
And if you but listen in the stillness of the night you shall hear them
    saying in silence,
"Our God, who art our winged self, it is thy will in us that willeth
It is thy desire in us that desireth.
It is thy urge in us that would turn our nights, which are thine, into
    days which are thine also.
We cannot ask thee for aught, for thou knowest our needs before they
    are born in us:
Thou art our need; and in giving us more of thyself thou givest
    us all.

— *Kahlil Gibran*

Kahlil Gibran's famous work, *The Prophet,* consistently interiorizes spiritual themes in language that is distinctly Christian. Gibran was raised in a Christian family in Lebanon. This poem challenges the conventional understanding of prayer as petition and says that true prayer, if it uses words at all, uses only those that are spoken through us by God. Otherwise prayer is silence and stillness in which we can hear the deepest prayer that is offered by the rest of Creation: Thy will be done in all things.

————◆————

Images, however sacred

Images, however sacred
they may be, retain
the attention outside,
whereas at the time of prayer
the attention must be within—
in the heart. The concentration
of attention in the heart—
this is the starting point of prayer.

— Saint Theophan the Recluse

Theophan, an Orthodox monk who lived in 19th-century Russia, reaffirms in these lines what Scott Cairns says in "Adventures in New Testament Greek: Nous": the prayer of the heart requires that we bring our attention down into the chest, into the deepest center of our person. That is the starting point. From there all else will be revealed.

———◆———

Unholy Sonnet 11

Half asleep in prayer I said the right thing
And felt a sudden pleasure come into
The room or my own body. In the dark,
Charged with a change of atmosphere, at first
I couldn't tell my body from the room.
And I was wide awake, full of this feeling,
Alert as though I'd heard a doorknob twist,
A drawer pulled, and instead of terror knew
The intrusion of an overwhelming joy.
I had said thanks and this was the response.
But how I said it or what I said it for
I still cannot recall and I have tried
All sorts of ways all hours of the night.
Once was enough to be dissatisfied.

— Mark Jarman

Mark Jarman's poems are a balm upon the brow. Heartfelt, personal, deep with insight, they do not preach but speak to the reader as confidant or friend. I love the tenderness in this poem—how he is not sure whether the pleasure filled his body or the room or both. It is a pleasure without location, known in a moment of waking, as if some unknown sound intrudes, though not as a terror but as an *overwhelming joy*.

———◆———

Descend from your head into your heart

You must descend from
your head into your heart.
At present your thoughts of God
are in your head. And God Himself is,
as it were, outside you, and
so your prayer and other spiritual
exercises
remain exterior. Whilst you are still
in your head,
thoughts will not easily be subdued but
will always be whirling about, like snow
in winter or
clouds of mosquitoes in summer.

— Saint Theophan the Recluse

Saint Diadochos of Photiki, an Orthodox monk whose writings are included in the *Philokalia,* makes it clear in these lines how prayer is not an affair of the mind. As long as we talk to God in our head alone, He remains external to us and our thoughts will continue to whirl about like mosquitoes. Our attention needs to descend into the heart, the center of our being, so that our prayer is authentic and not a mere litany of words.

———◆———

What is Grace?

"What is grace?" I asked God.

And He said,

"All that happens."

Then He added, when I looked perplexed,

"Could not lovers
say that every moment in their Beloved's arms
was grace?

Existence is my arms,
though I well understand how one can turn
away from
me

until the heart has
wisdom."

— *Saint John of the Cross*

In this rendering of the words of Saint John of the Cross, Daniel Ladinsky uses the metaphor of the lovers to put forward an idea that is not easy for most Westerners to identify with: everything that happens is grace, which is another way of saying that every event is not only good but also meant to happen. This may sound too much like fatalism for many, but the analogy of the lovers is a powerful argument: if we can experience everything that happens in our lover's arms as grace, then surely, if we could actually experience existence for what it is—the widespread arms of God—everything that happens in life must also be His grace. We will only realize this, though, when we have the wisdom to see that everything, our misfortunes as well as our blessings, comes from the same source.

————◆————

The Mysterious Place

*Saint Augustine says that there is a mysterious place
deep in the soul that is beyond time and this world, a part
higher than that which gives life and movement to
the body; true prayer so raises the heart that God can
come into this innermost place, the most disinterested,
intimate, and noble part of our being, the seat of our unity.
It is His eternal dwelling-place, and
into this grand and mysterious kingdom He pours
the sweet delight of which I have spoken. Then is man no
longer troubled by anything: he is recollected, quiet, and
really himself, and becomes daily more detached,
spiritualized, and contemplative, for God is within him,
reigning and working in the depths of his soul.*

— John Tauler

Johannes Tauler, one of the principal followers of Meister Eckhart, was a renowned preacher in 14th-century Germany. These lines are from a sermon he gave on true prayer. We must raise the heart, the center of our being, to a pitch or frequency that attracts God deep into our innermost soul—*the most disinterested, intimate, and noble part of our being, the seat of our unity.*

Disinterested means free of attachments, which makes it clear that the heart Tauler is speaking of does not concern the emotions but a depth of feeling which allows us to be intimate with life without being attached to it. This is our deepest human nature, in which we become truly ourselves.

———◆———

God's Grandeur

The world is charged with the grandeur of God.
    It will flame out, like shining from shook foil;
    It gathers to a greatness, like the ooze of oil
Crushed. Why do men then now not reck his rod?
Generations have trod, have trod, have trod;
    And all is seared with trade; bleared, smeared with toil;
    And wears man's smudge and shares man's smell: the soil
Is bare now, nor can foot feel, being shod.

And for all this, nature is never spent;
    There lives the dearest freshness deep down things;
And though the last lights off the black West went
    Oh, morning, at the brown brink eastward, springs—
Because the Holy Ghost over the bent
    World broods with warm breast and with ah! bright wings.

— Gerard Manley Hopkins

The language of Hopkins' sonnets may seem abstruse at first, but let the words and phrases roll around your mouth without trying to immediately grasp the sense of them; then his hallmark sprung rhythm and alliteration become incantatory and will draw you in the way a musical movement does.

The first octave tells us the world is permeated—*charged*—with God's energy, which flames out everywhere like electricity or lightning, and yet mankind lives on unaware of it.

Why do men then now not reck his rod?

Why, Hopkins wonders, do men not recognize his rod, his scepter, royal symbol of authority? Because they have lost touch with nature and are consumed with work.

The sextet then goes on to say that despite man's insensitive treatment of the world, nature can never be destroyed because of the inherent presence of God in all things. Despite the darkness, dawn will come again.

———◆———

As king fishers catch fire, dragon flies dráw fláme;

As kingfishers catch fire, dragonflies dráw fláme;
As tumbled over rim in roundy wells
Stones ring; like each tucked string tells, each hung bell's
Bow swung finds tongue to fling out broad its name;
Each mortal thing does one thing and the same:
Deals out that being indoors each one dwells;
Selves—goes itself; myself it speaks and spells,
Crying Whát I do is me: for that I came.
Í say móre: the just man justices;
Kéeps gráce: thát keeps all his goings graces;
Acts in God's eye what in God's eye he is—
Chríst—for Christ plays in ten thousand places,
Lovely in limbs, and lovely in eyes not his
To the Father through the features of men's faces.

— Gerard Manley Hopkins

Hopkins' rythmic alliteration is so strong in the first line of this glorious sonnet that it can have the effect of your favorite song: you may find it difficult to get out of your mind. The octave lays out creation for us and says that every single thing, even a stone tumbling down a *roundy well* (the poet is permitted to make up his own words!) sings out its true name with everything it does. The word *selves* in the seventh line is used as a verb—every mortal thing makes itself in everything it does.

The sextet addresses the human world in the same terms. The just man spreads his justice in the world simply by being who he is. Christ is the pure essence of who we are, and that essence—if only we have the eyes to see—shines out of every human face.

———◆———

A Blessing

May the light of your soul guide you.
May the light of your soul bless the work you do with the secret
*   love and warmth of your heart.*
May you see in what you do the beauty of your own soul.
May the sacredness of your work bring healing, light, and renewal
*   to those who work with you and to those who see and receive*
*   your work.*
May your work never weary you.
May it release within you wellsprings of refreshment, inspiration,
*   and excitement.*
May you be present in what you do.
May you never become lost in the bland absences.
May the day never burden.
May dawn find you awake and alert, approaching your new day
*   with dreams, possibilities, and promises.*
May evening find you gracious and fulfilled.
May you go into the night blessed, sheltered, and protected.
May your soul calm, console, and renew you.

— John O'Donohue

John O'Donohue's poem echoes the previous poem by Hopkins. The soul will be our true guide in everything if we allow it to show us the way. It will bless our work and those we meet; and it will protect us from *the bland absences*—a condition all of us suffer at one time or another. O'Donohue, an Irish Catholic priest who eventually left the priesthood to devote his time to writing, philosophy, and meditation, called the body the visible shoreline of the invisible world of the soul. And the soul, said O'Donohue, who died in 2008, is not in the body; rather the body is to be found in the soul.

———◆———

The Moor

It was like a church to me.
I entered it on soft foot,
Breath held like a cap in the hand.
It was quiet.
What God was there made himself felt,
Not listened to, in clean colours
That brought a moistening of the eye,
In movement of the wind over grass.

There were no prayers said. But stillness
Of the heart's passions—that was praise
Enough; and the mind's cession
Of its kingdom. I walked on,
Simple and poor, while the air crumbled
And broke on me generously as bread.

— R.S. Thomas

R.S. Thomas, a renowned Welsh poet, once said in a radio interview that in his poetry he was trying to find out what it means to use the word *God* in the late 20th century. This beautiful poem is an example of his effort. Thomas, a minister who wandered over the moors immersed in tranquility, makes a direct comparison between church and nature. The image at the end—

I walked on,
Simple and poor, while the air crumbled
And broke on me generously as bread

is a wonder, rich in its evocation of the sacrament of communion.

———◆———

The Morning Watch

O joys! Infinite sweetness! With what flowers
And shoots of glory, my soul breaks and buds!
    All the long hours
    Of night and rest,
    Through the still shrouds
    Of sleep, and clouds,
    This dew fell on my breast ;
    O how it bloods,
And spirits all my earth! Hark! In what rings,
And hymning circulations the quick world
    Awakes, and sings!
    The rising winds,
    And falling springs,
    Birds, beasts, all things
    Adore Him in their kinds.
    Thus all is hurled
In sacred hymns and order; the great chime
And symphony of Nature. Prayer is
    The world in tune,
    A spirit-voice,
    And vocal joys,
    Whose echo is heaven's bliss.
    O let me climb
When I lie down! The pious soul by night
Is like a clouded star, whose beams, though said
    To shed their light
    Under some cloud,
    Yet are above,
    And shine and move
    Beyond that misty shroud.
    So in my bed,
That curtain'd grave, though sleep, like ashes, hide
My lamp and life, both shall in Thee abide.

— Henry Vaughan

With what flowers
And shoots of glory my soul breaks and buds!

If ever there were a poem of ecstasy, this would be it. Henry Vaughan was one of the British metaphysical poets of the 17th century. His mystical conversion was inspired by the work of George Herbert, but while Herbert was a conformist in his adherence to the institution and dogma of the church, Vaughan was overtly mystical, describing his ecstatic states of communion with the Divine and the divinity of the natural world. The dew that fell on his breast is reminiscent of the Hindu amrit, the divine nectar that drips down into the heart from the crown of the head and signifies full awakening.

Prayer is the world in tune, the poet says, meaning not just the outer world but also the inner world of the human being—in tune with the ever-shining star of the soul, which is always reflecting the glory of God, no matter how many clouds may seem to obscure it.

———◆———

The Inner History of a Day (excerpt)

We seldom notice how each day is a holy place
Where the eucharist of the ordinary happens,
Transforming our broken fragments
Into an eternal continuity that keeps us.

Somewhere in us a dignity presides
That is more gracious than the smallness
That fuels us with fear and force,
A dignity that trusts the form a day takes.

So at the end of this day, we give thanks
For being betrothed to the unknown
And for the secret work
Through which the mind of the day
And wisdom of the soul become one.

— John O'Donohue

This is a wake-up-and-remember poem—a reminder that the day, the moment, we are living now is in itself a eucharist of the ordinary. In Christian terms, this moment, whatever it holds for us, is the body of Christ. When we absorb this truth, not just as a concept but also by being fully present to the moment, then we are made whole. In this wholeness lies our dignity as human beings.

———◆———

On Good and Evil (excerpt)

And one of the elders of the city said, Speak to us of Good and Evil.
And he answered:

. . . .

You are good when you are one with yourself.
Yet when you are not one with yourself you are not evil.
For a divided house is not a den of thieves; it is only a divided house
And a ship without rudder may wander aimlessly among perilous
 isles yet sink not to the bottom.

. . . .

In your longing for your giant self lies your goodness: and that
 longing is in all of you.
But in some of you that longing is a torrent rushing with might to
 the sea, carrying the secrets of the hillsides and the songs of
 the forest
And in others it is a flat stream that loses itself in angles and bends
 and lingers before it reaches the shore.
But let not him who longs much say to him who longs little,
 "Wherefore are you slow and halting?"
For the truly good ask not the naked, "Where is your garment?"
 nor the houseless, "What has befallen your house?"

— Kahlil Gibran

In this excerpt from *The Prophet,* Kahlil Gibran departs from the traditional dualistic view of Christianity that divides the affairs of the world and the soul of man into good and evil. He posits instead a more forgiving, unified perspective that treats evil like the Hindu or Buddhist traditions—as a condition of ignorance from which to awaken and for which there is no need for blame or judgment.

———◆———

How the Soul Through the Senses Finds God in All Creatures (excerpt)

O Love, divine Love, why do You lay siege to me?
In a frenzy of love for me, You find no rest.

From five sides You move against me,
Hearing, sight, taste, touch, and scent.
To come out is to be caught; I cannot hide from You.

If I come out through sight I see Love
Painted in every form and color,
Inviting me to come to You, to dwell in You.

If I leave through the door of hearing,
What I hear points only to You, Lord;
I cannot escape Love through this gate.

If I come out through taste, every flavor proclaims:
"Love, divine Love, hungering Love!
You have caught me on Your hook, for you want to reign in me."

If I leave through the door of scent
I sense You in all creation; You have caught me
And wounded me through that fragrance.

If I come out through the sense of touch
I find Your lineaments in every creature;
To try to flee from You is madness.

Love, I flee from You, afraid to give You my heart:
I see that You make me one with You,
I cease to be me and can no longer find myself.

— *Jacopone da Todi*

Brother Jacopone, a Franciscan who followed a radical form of poverty, was from Todi, a small town in central Italy. As this poem shows, he was an ecstatic whose love for God reached into every cell and sense organ of his body. He portrays himself here as God's quarry. By whichever sense he tries to come out, God is waiting for him. There is no escape, so he finally lets himself be filled so utterly by God that nothing of his own self remains.

———◆———

Pied Beauty

Glory be to God for dappled things—
   For skies of couple-colour as a brinded cow;
      For rose-moles all in stipple upon trout that swim;
Fresh-firecoal chestnut-falls; finches' wings;
   Landscape plotted and pieced—fold, fallow, and plough;
      And áll trádes, their gear and tackle and trim.
All things counter, original, spare, strange;
   Whatever is fickle, freckled (who knows how?)
      With swift, slow; sweet, sour; adazzle, dim;
He fathers-forth whose beauty is past change:
      Praise him.

— Gerard Manley Hopkins

Skies of couple-colour . . . fresh-firecoal chestnut-falls . . . the poem "Pied Beauty" is a joyous song of praise in which Hopkins uses his love of alliteration and compressed syntax in every line to celebrate both the infinite variety and beauty of nature and the incomprehensible mind of God who created it all. Hopkins wrote the poem in 1877, though, like the rest of his work, it was first published only 29 years after his death. It is for this reason that he is sometimes called an early modern poet, one who was far ahead of his Victorian times.

———◆———

On Reason and Passion (excerpt)

*And the priestess spoke again and said: Speak to us of Reason
and Passion.*
And he answered, saying:
. . . .
*Your reason and your passion are the rudder and the sails of
your seafaring soul.*
*If either your sails or your rudder be broken, you can but toss
and drift, or else be held at a standstill in mid-seas.*
*For reason, ruling alone, is a force confining; and passion,
unattended, is a flame that burns to its own destruction.*
*Therefore let your soul exalt your reason to the height of
passion, that it may sing;*
*And let it direct your passion with reason, that your
passion may live through its own daily resurrection,
and like the phoenix rise above its own ashes.*
. . . .
*Among the hills, when you sit in the cool shade of the
white poplars sharing the peace and serenity of distant
fields and meadows—then let your heart say in silence,
"God rests in reason."*
*And when the storm comes, and the mighty wind shakes
the forest, and thunder and lightning proclaim the majesty of the
sky,—then let your heart say in awe, "God moves in passion."*
*And since you are a breath in God's sphere, and a leaf
in God's forest, you too should rest in reason and move in passion.*
— Kahlil Gibran

Gibran seeks in his work to reconcile opposites. In this section of *The Prophet*, he addresses an issue that the Church as an institution has struggled with since its inception. He shows with his beautiful images how necessary both reason and passion, rightly used, are to the spiritual journey. Passion, or desire, is all too often seen as the enemy of spiritual practice and wisdom. In all traditions there is an emphasis on freedom from attachment to worldly things, which can be mistaken to suggest the mortification of the body and its appetites. Reason, on the other hand, can be seen as a deadener of the spirit, especially by those inclined to more emotional expressions of religion. Rest in reason and move in passion is the culminating wisdom of this passage.

———◆———

I Loved What I Could Love

I had a natural passion for fine clothes, excellent food, and
lively conversation about all matters that concern
the heart still alive. And even a passion
about my own
looks.

Vanities: they do not exist.

Have you ever walked across a stream stepping on
rocks so not to spoil a pair of shoes?

All we can touch, swallow, or say
aids in our crossing to God
and helps unveil the
soul.

Life smooths us, rounds, perfects, as does the river the stone,
and there is no place our Beloved is not flowing
though the current's force you
may not always
like.

Our passions help to lift us.

I loved what I could love until I held Him,
for then—all things—every world
disappeared.

— Saint Teresa of Ávila

There is no place our Beloved is not flowing: this is Saint Teresa's own celebration of the place and value of passion in our lives. She was one of the most passionate individuals the Church has ever known, so this should be good advice coming from her. Everything that we do and everything that happens in our lives has its place in our journey and is leading us to our destination, she says. Her passions for this and that—food, clothes, and conversation—were natural, she tells us. Nothing wrong with any of them. But when you fall in love with the real thing, it's only natural that your lesser loves fall away.

————◆————

Consumed in Grace

I first saw God when I was a child, six years of age.
The cheeks of the sun were pale before Him,
and the earth acted as a shy
girl, like me.

Divine light entered my heart from His love
that did never fully wane,

though indeed, dear, I can understand how a person's
faith can at times flicker,

for what is the mind to do
with something that becomes the mind's ruin:
a God that consumes us
in His grace.

I have seen what you want;
it is there,

a Beloved of infinite
tenderness.

— Saint Catherine of Siena

for what is the mind to do
with something that becomes the mind's ruin?

Catherine's ordinary mind was indeed brought to ruin when she was no more than six or seven years old. She had her first vision of Christ at that age, after which she took a vow of perpetual virginity. Nothing remains the same after an experience like that. Although her parents tried to steer her toward conventional marriage and a life of family, she joined the Dominican Order when she was 16 and for three years spoke to no one except her confessor, fasted, prayed, and stayed in her room. She continued to have visions throughout her life, and eventually she became highly active and influential in Church affairs and politics. She also spent a great deal of time caring for the poor and sick in her town.

———◆———

This Place of Abundance

We know nothing until we know everything.

I have no object to defend
for all is of equal value
to me.

I cannot lose anything in this
place of abundance
I found.

If something my heart cherishes
is taken away,

I just say, "Lord, what happened?"

And a hundred more appear.
— Saint Catherine of Siena

The law of abundance was discovered long before contemporary self-help books trumpeted it as a secret everyone should know. Except Saint Catherine's place of abundance starts with a different premise than the materialist advice so common today. Catherine, who was born in Siena, Italy, in 1347, has utterly abandoned herself to the love of her Lord. In that love, for which she has given up everything, everything is given to her. For he that hath, to him shall be given (Mark 4:25). In that love, all in this world is of equal value. She is utterly given to one love, and through that she is given whatever is needed. What a blessed state, costing not less than everything, as T.S. Eliot said.

———◆———

Those who are indignant

Those who are indignant at and rebel against
the things that befall them are blind with self-love.
I speak to you now in general and in particular, and
I say that they take for evil and regard as misfortunes, ruin,
evidence of hate towards themselves, the things that I
do out of love and for their good, that they may be
saved from eternal loss and receive the life that shall not
pass away. Why then do they murmur against Me? Because
they have put their trust in themselves, and so all becomes
dark for them and they do not know things as they are.

— Saint Catherine of Siena

This passage comes from Saint Catherine's work, *The Dialogue*, which like her many letters and other writings, was dictated under divine inspiration, much of which she received during mystical experiences. Christ is telling us that everything that happens to us, not just the joys but the sorrows too, comes from Him. Our great mistake is to put our trust in ourselves, which makes us see the world upside down.

———◆———

In Silence (excerpt)

Be still.
Listen to the stones of the wall.
Be silent, they try
To speak your

Name.
Listen
To the living walls.
Who are you?
Who
Are you? Whose
Silence are you?

Who (be quiet)
Are you (as these stones
Are quiet). Do not
Think of what you are
Still less of
What you may one day be.
Rather
Be what you are (but who?) be
The unthinkable one
You do not know.

— Thomas Merton

Thomas Merton evokes in this poem a question (Who are you?) that does not require an answer in words:

Who (be quiet)
Are you

It does not require any thinking at all, neither of what you are nor *What you one day may be.* Rather it requires us to be what we are, which is unthinkable, and to know through that being.

———◆———

The Prayer of Quiet

The soul, then, being thus inwardly recollected in
God or before God, now and then becomes so
sweetly attentive to the goodness of her well-beloved,
that her attention seems not to her to be attention, so
purely and delicately is it exercised; as it happens
to certain rivers, which glide so calmly and smoothly that
beholders and such as float upon them, seem neither to
see nor feel any motion, because the waters are not
seen to ripple or flow at all.

— *Saint Francis de Sales*

This fine insight into the nature of attention comes from Saint Francis de Sales' famous book, *An Introduction to the Devout Life*. De Sales believed that there comes a point in deep contemplation when you are no longer conscious of being a witness to an object of worship or devotion. You are no longer concentrating on something external to you but have merged in some way with the river of awareness—a vibrant, radiant stillness undisturbed by thought or feeling.

————◆————

God, whose love and joy

God, whose love and joy
  are present everywhere,
can't come to visit you
  unless you aren't there.

— Angelus Silesius

This is about as crisp and succinct as it gets: what has to disappear for us to know that love and joy are everywhere is not just the concept but also the sensation of being a separate entity of consciousness. Silesius is asserting in his own way that there is no separate self in reality. When we realize this as a felt knowledge—when self-consciousness itself dissolves—there is simply an awareness of the unity of things as they are. This awareness and delight are precisely the love and joy that the separate self wanted all along; however, it wanted these for itself, to claim as part of its identity. But this acquisition is not possible because awareness does not belong to anyone. When the ego doesn't try to make love and joy its own, they can just flow, and we become part of the flow.

———◆———

I Cobbled Their Boots

How could I love my fellow men who tortured me?

*One night I was dragged into a room
and beaten near death with
their shoes*

*striking me hundreds of times
in the face, scarring me
forever.*

I cried out for God to help, until I fainted.

*That night in a dream, in a dream more real than this world,
a strap from the Christ's sandal
fell from my bleeding
mouth,*

*and I looked at Him and He
was weeping, and
spoke,*

*"I cobbled their boots;
how sorry
I am.*

*What moves all things
is God."*

— *Saint John of the Cross*

This radical statement by Saint John is further affirmation of a difficult truth: everything that happens is of God, which means that even Hitler and Stalin were playing their part, as was Judas. This is in stark contrast to the dualistic perspective of the Gnostics, who believed that this world was created, not by God but by the forces of evil, which are somehow outside of God's sphere of influence. The same dualistic thinking occurs today when we wonder why bad things happen to good people—as if suffering were something some people deserved and others didn't, according to the brownie point tally on their score card. Suffering happens. It is heartbreaking; but ultimately, it is not personal.

The love of God, unutterable and perfect

"The love of God, unutterable and perfect,
   flows into a pure soul the way that light
   rushes into a transparent object.
The more love that it finds, the more it gives
   itself; so that, as we grow clear and open,
   the more complete the joy of heaven is.
And the more souls who resonate together,
   the greater the intensity of their love,
   and, mirror-like, each soul reflects the other."

— Dante Alighieri

Virgil is speaking these lines to Dante while they are traveling through Purgatory. A pure soul is like a transparent object. To the degree it is unobstructed by our egoic needs and demands, it can absorb the love of God. Our task is to grow clear and open, and the Purgatorio stage of Dante's journey is for just that purpose. It purifies him through healing fire and prepares him to be ready and able to gaze unflinchingly on the beauty he will find in Paradiso, the third and final part of the journey. Dante also says in this passage that as we keep company with pilgrims of like mind and heart, so our love will be deepened still further.

———◆———

But you who are so happy here

"But you who are so happy here, tell me:
  do you aspire to a more profound
  insight, or a greater ecstasy?"
She smiled a little, as did the shades beside her;
  then answered with such gladness that her whole
  being seemed to glow with love's first fire:
"Brother, God's generosity itself
  calms our will, and makes us want no more
  than what we have, and long for nothing else.
If we desired any greater bliss,
  we would not be in harmony with Him
  whose love assigns us to a lower place.
The essence of this joy is that we all
  have given up our personal desires
  so that our will is merged with God's own will.
Therefore our rank in heaven, from height to height,
  is just as dear to each particular soul
  as to the Master who appointed it.
In His will is our peace: it is the sea
  into which all currents and streams
  empty themselves, for eternity."

— Dante Alighieri

Dante speaks these lines to Piccarda Donati, one of the individuals he meets in Paradiso. There are levels of bliss in Paradiso, but everyone is completely content with the station they find themselves given. There is no envy of those on a higher level or superiority toward those lower on the scale. We are in Paradise, suggests Dante, when we accept our situation as it is and surrender our personal desires to God's will.

———◆———

But the silence in the mind

But the silence in the mind
is when we live best, within
listening distance of the silence
we call God. This is the deep
calling to deep of the psalm-
writer, the bottomless ocean
We launch the armada of
our thoughts on, never arriving.

It is a presence, then,
whose margins are our margins;
that calls us out over our
own fathoms. What to do
but draw a little nearer to
such ubiquity by remaining still?

— R.S. Thomas

R.S. Thomas, Welsh poet and Anglican clergyman who died in 2000, has written in these lines one of the most beautiful poems on silence that I know. Not merely an intellectual appreciation, his words are infused with a deeply felt experience of the sacred stillness. The phrase, to be

> *within*
> *listening distance of the silence*
> *we call God*

elegantly expresses the aim of the contemplative in barely more than a line.

———◆———

When we are weak

*When we are weak, we are
strong. When our eyes close
on the world, then somewhere
within us the bush
burns. When we are poor
and aware of the inadequacy
of our table, it is to that
uninvited the guest comes.*

— *R.S. Thomas*

Thomas's poems are always close to the ground and to nature, and are full of the motion of bowing down—not to this or that necessarily, but to the impossibility of our situation, to the fact of our fault lines. It is humility that brings us close to the ground and that helps us laugh at ourselves. No accident, then, that the word *humility* has the same root as *humus* and *humor*. Life is a paradox, and neither it nor we are ever quite what we seem. Strangely, in our humility lies our strength; when we bow down, we are raised up. There is a bush that burns somewhere within us when our eyes close on the world. When we least expect it, grace can open the door.

———◆———

The Fall (excerpt)

There is no where in you a paradise that is no place and there
You do not enter except without a story.

To enter there is to become unnameable.
. . . .
Whoever is nowhere is nobody, and therefore cannot exist
  except unborn:
No disguise will avail him anything

Such a one is neither lost nor found.

But he who has an address is lost.
. . . .
Who would dare to go nameless in so secure a universe?
Yet, to tell the truth, only the nameless are at home in it.

They bear with them in the center of nowhere the unborn
  flower of nothing:
This is the paradise tree. It must remain unseen until words
  end and arguments are silent.

— *Thomas Merton*

Merton here is abstract, brilliant, and challenging. He uses a persistent rain of short sharp words to impress upon us that our personal story—the drama through time of who we think we are—is precisely what has to fall away if we are ever, along with Dante, to enter Paradise, which is nowhere if not inside us, somewhere that can never be pointed to. Only the nameless are at home in the universe, Merton says.

———◆———

The Fountain (excerpt)

How well I know that flowing spring
  in black of night.

The eternal fountain is unseen.
How well I know where she has been
  in black of night.

I do not know her origin.
None. Yet in her all things begin
  in black of night.

I know that nothing is so fair
and earth and firmament drink there
  in black of night.

I know that none can wade inside
to find her bright bottomless tide
  in black of night.
. . . .
The eternal fountain is unseen
in living bread that gives us being
  in black of night.

She calls on all mankind to start
to drink her water, though in dark,
  for black is night.

O living fountain that I crave,
in bread of life I see her flame
  in black of night.

— Saint John of the Cross

The fountain of life never stops flowing. It is the invisible source of all visible forms. In the Christian tradition it is commonly associated with the Virgin Mary, the virgin mother of God in human form and by implication the mother of all things. The water of life is a current that can only be known in the darkness that comes when the mind is without thought. There in that darkness, and only there, John of the Cross sees what cannot be seen, the source of all light and life. The silent mind, far from being a barren emptiness, becomes radiant, brimming with the waters of eternal life that sustain the earth and firmament.

——◆——

A case of contradictories

A case of contradictories, both of them true.
There is a God. There is no God.
Where is the problem? I am quite sure that
there is a God in the sense that I am
sure my love is no illusion. I am quite sure
there is no God, in the sense that I am sure
there is nothing which resembles what
I can conceive when I say that word.

— Simone Weil

In this passage Simone Weil shows how paradox is fundamental to the nature of spiritual reality. Belief or dogma that insists on one certitude and denies any reality to its opposite confines us to only one version of the story. If there is a God, then she must exist in the ground of our experience, known to us intimately, rather than as some external form separate from ourselves. And yet is God, then, without existence except for us? I don't think so; but paradox defies all thinking.

————◆————

Unholy Sonnet 1

Dear God, Our Heavenly Father, Gracious Lord,
Mother Love and Maker, Light Divine,
Atomic Fingertip, Cosmic Design,
First letter of the Alphabet, Last Word,
Mutual Satisfaction, Cash Award,
Auditor Who Approves Our Bottom Line,
Examiner Who Says That We Are Fine,
Oasis That All Sands Are Running Toward.

I can say almost anything about you,
O Big Idea, and with each epithet,
Create new reasons to believe or doubt you,
Black Hole, White Hole, Presidential Jet.
But what's the anything I must leave out? You
Solve nothing but the problems that I set.

— Mark Jarman

What vibrant humor Mark Jarman gives us in this poem. He uses the language and images of our time to show the impossibility of being able to capture the essence of the Big Idea that, for want of a better term, we call God. He also reminds us that the only problems we have are the ones that we set ourselves.

———◆———

Unsophisticated teachers say

*Unsophisticated teachers say that God is pure
being. He is as high above being as the highest
angel is above a gnat. I would be speaking as incorrectly
in calling God a being as if I called the sun pale or black.
God is neither this nor that.*

— Meister Eckhart

Eckhart is saying essentially the same thing Mark Jarman does in "Unholy Sonnet 1," only in 14th-century language: *God is neither this nor that,* which also happens to be a translation of the Sanskrit Vedanta term, *neti neti.* He means that the mystery of God can never be pointed to with this or that explanation; it can never be understood or arrived at by logic. Religion, culture, and even time do not obscure what seem to be universal insights.

———◆———

As we climb higher

As we climb higher, we say this.
It is not soul or mind, nor does it possess
imagination, conviction, speech or understanding.

. . . .

It does not live nor is it life. It is not a
substance, nor is it eternity or time.

. . . .

It is not wisdom.
It is neither one nor oneness, divinity nor goodness.

. . . .

It falls neither within the predicate of nonbeing nor being.

. . . .

It is beyond assertion and denial. We make assertions and
denials of what is next to it, but never of it, for it is both beyond
every assertion, being the perfect and unique cause of all things,
and by virtue of its pre-eminently simple and absolute nature,
free of every limitation,
beyond every limitation;
it is also beyond every denial.

— Pseudo-Dionysius

Pseudo-Dionysius, also known as Dionysius the Areopagite, was the first great exponent in Christianity of via negativa theology. Eckhart, John of the Cross, Ruysbroek, and other later writers drew from his sources and inspiration. He essentially espouses—probably without knowing it—the Vedanta notion of neti neti (not this, not that). If we can point to the "truth" or name it, we can be sure that it is not truth. All dogmas, his own included, cannot begin to approach the Mystery.

———◆———

Upon a certain time

Upon a certain time when I was at prayer and my spirit was exalted,
God spake unto me many gracious words full of love.

And when I looked, I beheld God who spake with me.
But if thou seekest to know that which I beheld,
I can tell thee nothing,
save that I beheld a fullness and a clearness,
and felt them within me so abundantly that I can in no wise describe it,
nor give any likeness thereof.
For what I beheld was not corporal,
but as though it were in heaven.
Thus I beheld a beauty so great that I can say naught concerning it,
save that I saw the Supreme Beauty,
containeth within Itself all goodness.
And all the saints were standing before this beauteous Majesty,
praising it.

— Angela of Foligno

Angela of Foligno's words are remarkable, not only for their soaring inspiration but also for fusing both negating and positive language into one passage and giving us something that is somehow more exalted than either. She beheld God, but she could not begin to tell us what she saw. What she saw was within her and yet not corporeal. She saw the *Supreme Beauty,* but like Pseudo-Dionysius, she could say nothing about it, except that it was a fullness and a clearness. Angela was the wife of a 13th-century Umbrian nobleman. She fully indulged in the pleasures of life before giving up everything to follow the way of Saint Francis. The words she uttered in ecstasy, including these lines, were written down by a Friar Arnold.

———◆———

When He told me

When He told me that He concealed much love,
because I was not able to bear it, my soul answered:
"If Thou art God omnipotent, make Thou me able to bear it."

Then he made answer finally and said: "If I were to do as thou
askest, thou wouldst have
here all that thou desirest, and wouldst no longer hunger
after Me. For this reason I will not grant thy request, for
I desire that in this world thou shouldst hunger and long
after Me and shouldst ever be eager to find me."

— Angela of Foligno

Every lover longs to be united with the beloved, and for some the longing is preferable to the union itself. In fact the longing is a sign of union, and this is what God tells Angela of Foligno in her ecstasy—that the fire burning in her heart is the gift she has been waiting for. It concentrates the mind and burns away all other loves, leaving only the one. The goal here is the journey itself, not the arriving.

———◆———

The Dark Night (excerpt)

In the delicious night,
In privacy, where no one saw me,
Nor did I see one thing,
I had no light or guide
But the fire that burned inside my chest.

That fire showed me
The way more clearly than the blaze of noon
To where, waiting for me,
Was the One I knew so well,
In that place where no one ever is.

I stood still; I forgot who I was,
My face leaning against Him,
Everything stopped, abandoned me,
My being was gone, forgotten
Among the white lilies.

— Saint John of the Cross

Here is another ecstatic tribute to the deep interior passion of the spiritual lover—but one with a different outcome. The metaphor of lover and beloved expresses both a yearning for fulfillment and, at the same time, an intimation of a union that you sense is already, somehow, your natural state. You cannot want what you do not in some way already know. Saint John's famous love song is one that reaches its destination. Its joy is less in the seeking than in the finding. The poet is yearning no longer. The mood is tender and quiet; Saint John is finally at rest, for he has arrived.

The white lilies in the last line are a reference to the Resurrection, which in this context means the new life he finds in union with the Beloved.

———◆———

Wouldst thou know my meaning?

Wouldst thou know my meaning?
Lie down in the Fire
See and taste the Flowing
Godhead through thy being;
Feel the Holy Spirit
Moving and compelling
Thee within the Flowing
Fire and Light of God.

— *Mechtild of Magdeburg*

These lines come from Mechtild's great work, *The Flowing Light of the Godhead*, which James Harpur, in his book *Love Burning in the Soul*, calls "a masterpiece of visions, prayers, allegories, reflective pieces, and aphorisms, written in prose and verse." She was one of the great voices of German mysticism in the 13th century, as well as a lyric poet of the highest order.

Mechtild received many cosmic visions during which her soul left her body and she was able to see the world to come, as well as the shining figure of Jesus and the Holy Trinity. The main theme of her writings is the longing of the lover for the beloved, along with the necessity of the purging force of suffering and the practice of virtue.

In using images like *Lie down in the fire* and *the Flowing Light and Fire of God*, Mechtild is describing her own interior experience, and it is hard to miss the parallels with descriptions of kundalini to be found in classic yogic texts. Kundalini is the ecstatic, fiery energy that Yogic practitioners seek to draw up from the base of the spine to the crown of the head. Divine union, or marriage, for the yogi occurs when this happens, and the metaphor of lover and beloved is often used to describe the process.

———◆———

I cannot dance, O Lord

I cannot dance, O Lord,
Unless You lead me.
If You wish me to leap joyfully,
Let me see You dance and sing—

Then I will leap into Love—
And from Love into Knowledge,
And from Knowledge into the Harvest,
That sweetest Fruit beyond human sense.

There I will stay with You, whirling.

— Mechtild of Magdeburg

Mechtild describes in these lines her spiraling way of ascent to the Beloved and beyond. First, nothing can happen by her own will, only by the will of her Lord. By His will she is filled with love, from which grows knowledge (of other dimensions, perhaps) which moves into ecstasy, and finally she passes beyond human sensations altogether. Yet even in this rarified state beyond the body, she is aware that there are higher dimensions calling her onward, for it seems the journey is never ending.

————◆————

Thought is no longer of worth to me

Thought is no longer of worth to me,
Nor work, nor speech.
Love draws me so high
(Thought is no longer of worth to me)
With her divine gaze,
That I have no intent.
Thought is no longer of worth to me.
Nor work, nor speech.

— Marguerite Porete

For several hundred years from the end of the 13th century, an anonymous mystical text called *Mirror of Simple Souls* circulated around Europe, describing the stages of the soul's ascent to God. In 1946 it was finally determined that the book's author was Marguerite Porete, who was burned at the stake in Paris in 1310 for heresy.

Her book was based on dialogues between the figures of Love, Soul, Reason, and others, though it also includes poems and extended prose pieces.

For Porete, the human will is the primary obstacle to divine union, and in this belief she precedes *The Divine Comedy,* whose characters in the Paradiso say as much to Dante. Neither good works, nor reason, nor even the sacraments or the virtues can take the soul where only love can lead. Abiding in love the soul dissolves into the Trinity and becomes incapable of sin. None of this endeared Porete to the authorities, whom she openly criticized.

———◆———

Place your mind before the mirror of eternity

Place your mind before the mirror of eternity!
Place your soul in the brilliance of glory!
Place your heart in the figure of the divine substance!
And transform your whole being into the image of the
  Godhead Itself
    through contemplation!
So that you too may feel what His friends feel
    as they taste the hidden sweetness
    which God Himself has reserved
    from the beginning
    for those who love Him.

— Saint Clare of Assisi

It is said that Saint Clare of Assisi would come from prayer with her face so shining that it would dazzle everyone around her. Unlike Saint Francis, who advocated a life of service to the poor, Clare's enclosed community dedicated itself to contemplation. These lines tell us their aim: the transformation of the entire being into the image of the Godhead. The idea of an enclosed order of women was almost unthinkable at the time, especially one dedicated to strict poverty and contemplation; and like many mystical communities in the Middle Ages, Clare's ran the constant risk of admonishment by the church authorities.

———◆———

Ask Anything

"Ask anything,"

My Lord said to me.

*And my mind and heart thought deeply
for a second,*

then replied with just one word,

"When?"

*God's arms then opened up and I entered Myself.
I entered Myself when I entered
Christ.*

*And having learned compassion I
allowed my soul*

to stay.

— Saint Thomas Aquinas

Thomas Aquinas is more commonly known as the greatest of all Catholic theologians, rather than as a mystic and contemplative, and near the end of his life he received a divine revelation while celebrating mass in Naples. This revelation led him to say, "I can no longer write, for God has given me such glorious knowledge that all contained in my works are as straw . . . " Three months later, in 1274, he died.

In this poem he asks, *When? When will I be united with You?* And the answer comes from the pen of a mystic, not that of a theologian. For God's arms opened up and he entered his own Self; which, he goes on to say, is none other than Christ. Christ identified as your own essence is the foundational revelation of the Christian mystic.

———◆———

Unto this Darkness

*Unto this Darkness which is
beyond Light
we pray that we may come, and
may attain unto vision through
the loss of sight and knowledge,
and that in ceasing thus to see or
to know
we may learn to know that which
is beyond all perception and
understanding
(for this emptying of
our faculties
is true sight and knowledge).*

— *Pseudo-Dionysius*

These lines play with paradox to help us slip through the linear and rational processes of our own mind. We seek not the light but the darkness, but we must pass through and beyond the light to reach that darkness—beyond thinking and beyond imagining what we see to be true. Beyond dogma, then, and beyond fixed beliefs; beyond even our own inner images and insights, beyond perception and understanding altogether. In that darkness our habitual identity can no longer exist, and what we cannot know or even imagine is able to flower.

—◆—

Effortlessly

Effortlessly,
Love flows from God into man,
Like a bird
Who rivers the air
Without moving her wings.
Thus we move in His world
One in body and soul,
Though outwardly separate in form.
As the Source strikes the note,
Humanity sings—
The Holy Spirit is our harpist,
And all the strings
Which are touched in Love
Must sound.

— Mechtild of Magdeburg

Like a bird in the air or a fish in water we live and breathe and move in God's love always, whether we know it or not. So there is nowhere to seek and nothing to do except to recognize and bow to that which is already so. Then our life is as effortless as a bird that rivers the air.

———◆———

A fish cannot drown in water

A fish cannot drown in water,
A bird does not fall in air.
In the fire of its making,
Gold doesn't vanish:
The fire brightens.
Each creature God made
Must live in its own true nature;
How could I resist my nature,
That lives for oneness with God?

— *Mechtild of Magdeburg*

The love of God is the air Mechtild of Magdeburg breathes. It is not a discipline or a practice, it is her most intimate experience of being alive, like breathing itself. But while she may or may not be aware of her physical breath, she is profoundly conscious of this love that moves through her constantly. In this way she is joined to it, one with it; though it is not clear in this translation whether it is the longing for union she experiences in this way or the union itself. But as we have seen elsewhere in this collection, the longing and the union are ultimately the same.

———◆———

And therefore I am unborn

And therefore I am unborn, and
in the manner in which I am
unborn
I can never die.
. . . .
In my birth all things were
born
and I was the cause of myself
and of all things; and
if I would have wished it,
I would not be nor would all other things
be.
And if I did not exist,
"God" would also not exist.
That God is "God,"
of that I am a cause;
if I did not exist, God
too would not be "God."
There is no need
to understand
this.

— Meister Eckhart

Eckhart is always striving to articulate the impossible: what is beyond all words and concepts, even the concept of God. The title of this passage, "And therefore I am unborn," calls to mind the image of our "original face" that is frequently used in Buddhism to evoke the purity and innocence of what we are and what we were before we developed a personal self and sense of separateness.

Poverty for Eckhart was a quality of spirit rather than any act of external renunciation, and this internal poverty requires—as it did also for Marguerite Porete—that "a poor man wants nothing, knows nothing, and has nothing." He means that one should not even want to do God's will, so that one is as empty of God as of anything else; that one should fall away from all knowledge, even including the knowing that God lives in you; and that in having nothing, one should not even have a place where God can work in you.

If this occurs, we would not exist as we normally know ourselves, and God—a construct of our own mind—would not exist either. Everything, including God, only comes into being when our own separate self comes into being and we see with eyes that set us apart from everything else. Eckhart is pointing to a condition of radical unity that cannot affirm in any way the existence of a subject/object relationship.

———◆———

But in the breaking-through

But in the breaking-through, when
I come to be free of
will of myself and of
God's will
and of all his works and
of God himself,
then I am above all
created things, and
I am neither God nor
creature,
but I am what I was and
what I shall remain, now and
eternally.
. . . .
I receive such riches that
God, as he is "God," and
as he performs all his
divine works,
cannot suffice me; for in
this breaking-through I
receive
that God and I
are one.

— Meister Eckhart

It is not surprising, reading passages like this, that Eckhart came close to being branded a heretic. For Eckhart, what lay beyond God was the Godhead—the God beyond God which is the simple, quiet no-thingness that the soul in its ground is always in union with. Salvation, as such, is a release of the personal will into the spaciousness of the no-thing that is both within and without us. What remains is blissful awareness without a witness or an object.

———◆———

The inward stirring

The inward stirring and
touching of God
makes us hungry and yearning;
for the Spirit of God hunts
our spirit;
and the more it touches it,
the greater our hunger
and our craving.
And this is the life of love in
its highest working,
above reason and above
understanding;
for reason can here neither
give nor take away from
love,
for our love is touched
by the Divine Love.

— Blessed John Ruysbroeck

Ruysbroeck was the great 14th-century Flemish mystic who shared a similar outlook with Eckhart and Tauler, the Rhineland mystics of the same era. He died in 1381 at the age of 88, after a lifetime of deep contemplation and mystical union with God. These lines echo those of Saint Augustine, when he speaks of the soul, once having been touched by the love of God, yearning and longing for nothing else.

———◆———

Indescribable vastness

Indescribable vastness,
streaming from all sides,
streaming from no sides,
an ocean full and overflowing
with a luminous nothing.

. . . .
where no word has ever gone, but
out of which the Word emerges.
And so this Silence washes
onto the shores of perception,
making it stretch to receive
in metaphors of light,
union, calm,
spaciousness.

. . . .
You are the vastness
into which you gaze.
"Deep calls unto deep in the
roar of your waters" (Ps 42:7).

— Martin Laird

Martin Laird is a poet who happens to write in prose. This beautiful passage is typical of the dignified passion that informs *Into the Silent Land,* Laird's book on the Christian practice of contemplation. It is clear from his book that Laird is not only an academic but also someone who has in-depth experience of Christian contemplation, as well as meditative practices from other traditions.

———◆———

What is this wondrous mystery

What is this wondrous mystery
unfolding within me?
I have no words to name it,
for that One is above all praise,
transcends all words
my reason sees what has happened,
wishes to explain,
yet can find no words to tell you.
What it sees is invisible,
simple, pure,
unbounded in its majesty.
I have seen the totality,
received not in essence
but by participation.
As when you light a flame from a flame,
the whole flame you receive.

— *Saint Symeon the New Theologian*

The wondrous mystery that Saint Symeon speaks of here is unfolding, not outside, but inside his body and mind. This is why he receives the gift of mystery through participation. His whole being is lit up so that it is identical in its totality to the flame (of God) that is doing the lighting. His reason sees what is happening; he is conscious and aware as he is participating, but what is unfolding in him remains far beyond the reach of words, even the words of poetry.

———◆———

For He is the Very Rest

For He is the Very Rest.
God wishes to be known,
And it pleases Him that
We rest in Him;
For all that is beneath Him
Will never satisfy us.
Therefore no soul is rested
Til it is emptied of all things
That are made.
When, for love of Him,
It is empty,
The soul can
Receive His deep rest.

— Julian of Norwich

The word *rest* is not one that has occurred in the other poems in this book, yet it is a central theme in Christian contemplation. "Be still and know that I am God," the Psalmist says (Psalm 46:10); yet the word *rest* adds another dimension to the stillness. It implies letting go of effort—even the effort to be internally still—and allowing oneself to be held by something that may be intuited but can never be named or known. When we finally let go of all desires for this and that, when we are empty, we can

Receive His deep rest.

Resting in Him, we shall want for nothing.

———◆———

Self-Annihilation and Charity Lead... (excerpt)

As air becomes the medium for light when the sun rises,
And as wax melts from the heat of fire,
So the soul drawn to that light is resplendent,
Feels self melt away,
Its will and actions no longer its own.
So clear is the imprint of God
That the soul, conquered, is conqueror;
Annihilated, it lives in triumph.

What happens to the drop of wine
That you pour into the sea?
Does it remain itself, unchanged?
It is as if it never existed.
So it is with the soul: Love drinks it in,
It is united with Truth,
Its old nature fades away,
It is no longer master of itself.

The soul wills and yet does not will:
Its will belongs to Another.
It has eyes only for this beauty;
It no longer seeks to possess, as was its wont—
It lacks the strength to possess such sweetness.
The base of this highest of peaks
Is founded on nichil,
Shaped into nothingness, made one with the Lord.

— Jacopone da Todi

All individuality is lost in this soaring song of a poem—lost in the love of God, in which it dissolves like a drop of wine in the ocean. Jacopone da Todi departs from Christian orthodoxy with this image, implying as it does that no trace is left of the individual once he is wholly absorbed in the ocean of consciousness that is God.

———◆———

Immersion

There is anger abroad in the world, a numb thunder,
because of God's silence. But how naive,
to keep wanting words we could speak ourselves,
English, Urdu, Tagalog, the French of Tours,
the French of Haiti ...
 Yes, that was one way omnipotence chose
to address us—Hebrew, Aramaic, or whatever the patriarchs
chose in their turn to call what they heard. Moses
demanded the word, spoken and written. But perfect freedom
assured other ways of speech. God is surely
patiently trying to immerse us in a different language,
events of grace, horrifying scrolls of history
and the unearned retrieval of blessings lost for ever,
the poor grass returning after drought, timid, persistent.
God's abstention is only from human dialects. The holy voice
utters its woe and glory in myriad musics, in signs and portents.
Our own words are for us to speak, a way to ask and to answer.

— Denise Levertov

Why is this poem called "Immersion," I wonder? Perhaps because the call and response of question and answer implies a subject/object relationship which can separate us, however subtly, from the One we want answers from. Whereas if we fall down and kiss the grass, *the grass returning after drought,* we bring an end to the drought caused in us by our separation from the world. We immerse ourselves in the world and are surrounded and enveloped in all the answers we could ever wish for; if only we open our eyes and ears to the *myriad musics* that *the holy voice* is continually speaking in.

———◆———

The Voice of the Devil

All Bibles or sacred codes, have been the causes of the following Errors:

1. That Man has two real existing principles Viz: a Body & a Soul.

2. That Energy, call'd Evil, is alone from the Body, & that Reason, call'd Good, is alone from the Soul.

3. That God will torment Man in Eternity for following his Energies.

But the following Contraries to these are True:

1. Man has no body distinct from his Soul for that call'd Body is a portion of Soul discern'd by the five Senses, the chief inlets of Soul in this age.

2. Energy is the only life and is from the Body and Reason is the bound or outward circumference of Energy.

3. Energy is Eternal Delight.

— William Blake

The body does not house the soul, Blake tells us; rather the *Body is a portion of Soul.* Energy, or desire, connects us to the living world and to each other and is thus *Eternal Delight.* The senses are the avenues that join us not only to the visible world but also to the beauty behind and beyond it. In another well-known passage from the same text, Blake says that

If the doors of perception were cleans'd
Everything would appear to man as it is, infinite.

———◆———

Praying

It doesn't have to be
the blue iris, it could be
weeds in a vacant lot, or a few
small stones; just
pay attention, then patch

a few words together and don't try
to make them elaborate, this isn't
a contest but the doorway

into thanks, and a silence in which
another voice may speak.

— Mary Oliver

As always, Mary Oliver's preferred place of reverence and prayer is the natural world. But the object of contemplation does not have to be one of nature's jewels, the blue iris, for example; a few weeds or small stones will do. What matters is to pay attention—her constant refrain—and to have your prayer as simple as the stones or weeds themselves. The prayer's purpose is to draw you toward a felt gratitude, which in turn leads to the silence in which you feel that the prayer is praying you, not the other way around.

———◆———

about the poets

Angela of Foligno (1248–1309)
Angela's story is one of classic redemption. She was married to an Umbrian nobleman, had several children with him, and at the same time had various affairs, resulting in the loss of her husband and children. She then vowed herself to a life of poverty and care of the sick as a Franciscan. She suffered a "dark night of the spirit" for two years, during which she would try and counteract her violent sensual desires by holding fire to her flesh. Her sufferings were followed by many mystical graces, and many eventually gathered round her to follow her spiritual counsel. The words she uttered in ecstasy were written down by her confessor, Friar Arnold.

Dante Alighieri (1265–1321)
Dante, a native of Florence, fell in love while still a youth with a girl named Bice di Folco Portinari, whom he subsequently referred to in his works as Beatrice, the muse of his entire lifetime. Beatrice died quite young, though while she was still alive Dante married Gemma Donati, with whom he had three children. He entered Florentine politics and allied himself with a party that fell from grace, which resulted in his being exiled from his native city for the rest of his life. He never returned and was given refuge in various Italian cities, eventually dying in Ravenna; not, however, before writing his masterpiece *The Divine Comedy,* one of the greatest achievements in all European literature.

Saint Thomas Aquinas (1225–1274)
Thomas was born to a noble family in Roccasecca in Italy. When he was five he was sent to the Benedictine Abbey of Monte Cassino to receive his basic education, with the family's expectation that he would become an abbot. He shocked his teachers with the profundity of his questions and insights about God, and from the earliest age showed a great love of the scriptures. When he was 17 he moved to the Dominican mendicant order, which at the time was considered countercultural, with its emphasis on poverty and absolute faith. His family kidnapped him and kept him in the family castle for two years in an attempt to make him disavow the Order, but he refused, and they eventually relented. After further studies in Naples he was appointed a master at the University of Paris in 1256, and it was during this time that he discovered and taught the long suppressed Aristotelian texts on metaphysics. Aristotle influenced him to see that all creation was a revelation of God's Being. Over the next 16 years he wrote nearly 100 remarkable works, while still managing to fall into frequent and deep states of contemplation.

W. H. Auden (1907–1973)

W. H. Auden was born in York, England, the last of three sons to a medical psychologist and a mother who was a devout Anglican. At Oxford he formed The Oxford Group of poets with Stephen Spender, Louis MacNeice, and others, to break with the poetic forms of the Victorian past and develop T.S. Eliot's modernist style, with its concrete images and free verse. *The Orators,* his second volume of poetry, was published when he was 21, and it set the mood for a generation of educated young men who were in revolt against the principles and values of the British Empire. In 1939 he emigrated to the USA, taught at various universities, and by the time he became an American citizen in 1946 he had a successful literary career. After a period as an atheist, he returned to the Anglican church in 1940, and his Christian faith became deeply infused in his work from then on.

Saint Augustine (354–430)

Augustine was born in the Roman province that is now Algeria. His father was a pagan and his mother a devout Christian, who brought him up in the faith. At the age of 17 he went off to study in Carthage, in what is now Tunisia, fathered an illegitimate child and generally led a somewhat dissolute life. In 383 he went to teach in Rome, and then in Milan, where he studied Neoplatonism and also heard the teachings of the charismatic Bishop Ambrose, who finally converted him to Christianity in 386. Back in North Africa, he became first a priest and then Bishop of Hippo in 396, a position he was to hold for 34 years, until his death. It was in Hippo that Augustine wrote his great works of theology, his *Confessions*—the first example of autobiography—and polemics against those he felt threatened the unity and doctrine of the church.

William Blake (1757–1827)

Poet, mystic, painter, and printmaker, William Blake was born in London into a family that encouraged his artistic talent from an early age. At the age of 21 he became a professional engraver, and in 1782 he married a poor illiterate girl, Catherine Boucher, whom he taught to read and write, as well as to engrave. His first collection of poems, *Poetical Sketches,* was published in 1783. Blake believed that the truth was revealed, not taught, and accordingly he allowed his own visions to guide both his life and work. He believed himself to be a prophet of a New Age and championed free love and democracy. His best-known poem is "Jerusalem." He struggled financially all his life, and was buried, penniless, in an unmarked grave. His life and belief can be summed up in his own words: "The Imagination is not a State: it is the Human Existence itself."

Scott Cairns (1954–)

Scott Cairns was born in Tacoma, Washington, into a Baptist family. As an adult he has developed a career teaching American literature and creative writing, as well as becoming a well-known Christian poet. On the inspiration of members of that faith whom he later met in his home state, he joined the Orthodox Church, and his poetry has since become imbued with the questions and epiphanies aroused in him as a result. Critics have said that he retrieves some of the important subject matter and moral urgency long ceded to prose writers. The Divine Liturgy and also the practice of the Jesus Prayer (the subject of his poem included in this volume) are at the heart of his spiritual life.

Saint Catherine of Siena (1347–1380)

The last of 24 children born to a cloth dyer and his wife in Siena, Italy, Catherine had her first vision at the age of six, and took a perpetual vow of virginity. Her parents wanted her to lead a conventional life, but at the age of 16 she joined the Dominicans as a lay sister, remaining at home, where she confined herself to her room for three years except for Mass, speaking to no one but her confessor. Then in 1366 she received a vision of her mystical marriage to Christ, which was also a summons to take up an active life of service inspired by Christ's love. She cared for lepers and for the sick, and she visited hospitals and prisons. She attracted many followers from all sections of society, thus becoming the "mother" of a large family of people dedicated to doing God's work with the poor. When another vision told her to engage more widely in the world, she dictated letters to popes and kings and princes. She persuaded the pope to return his court from Avignon to Rome and became involved in the struggle between the papacy and Florence. Her teachings are found in her work, *The Dialogue,* consisting of exchanges between her soul and God.

Jean Pierre de Caussade (1675–1751)

Jean Pierre de Caussade was born in France and at the age of 18 joined the Jesuit order in Toulouse. He became a successful teacher and preacher in Toulouse. In 1729, when he was 54, he moved to Lorraine and became spiritual director to nuns of the Visitation in the town of Nancy. His letters to the nuns were published in a book called *Abandonment to Divine Providence,* which established his reputation as a deeply perceptive spiritual thinker. He worked to show that contemplative prayer—the key to which, in his view, was summed up in the title of his book—was in fact supported by the traditional teachings of the church. Unconditional surrender to God meant for him the deep acceptance of whatever situation we find ourselves in, moment to moment.

Saint Clare of Assisi (1194–1253)

When Clare was nearly 18, she heard a sermon by Saint Francis of Assisi and vowed herself to a life of poverty. Her wealthy family brought her home by force, but she slipped back to the community of Saint Francis;

he cut off her hair and placed her in a convent. Later, a house was found for her, and she was soon joined by two of her sisters, her best friend, her widowed mother, and several members of a noble Florentine family. They became known as the Poor Clares and adopted a life of extreme austerity and absolute poverty. They had no beds, ate very little, and begged for whatever they needed. Clare always fasted more than anyone else. She and Francis developed a deep spiritual friendship over the years. The Poor Clares exist to this day in communities around the world.

Saint John of the Cross (1542–1591)
Saint John of the Cross was born in Old Castile, Spain, the youngest son of a silk weaver. He joined the Carmelite Order in 1563, and on meeting Saint Teresa of Ávila, agreed with her to initiate a reform order, The Discalced Carmelites. He was imprisoned in Toledo for his efforts, and it was in his cell that he began his work as a poet. His book *The Ascent of Mt. Carmel* is one of the greatest of Christian spiritual treatises to map the progress of the soul. It was written as a commentary on his poem "The Dark Night." Saint John of the Cross is known as one of the greatest Christian mystics of all time.

Saint Diadochos (c. 400–486)
Diadochos was Bishop of Photiki in Northern Greece. His 100 chapters on Spiritual Knowledge and Discrimination were described by Saint Nikodimos, one of the compilers of *The Philokalia,* as revealing "the deepest secrets of the virtues of prayer." His works, included in *The Philokalia,* were a great influence on later ascetics such as John Climacus and Saint Symeon the New Theologian. He was probably one of *the* Greek notables who were captured in a Vandal raid sometime around 470, taken to North Africa, near Carthage, and released, never to be seen or heard from again. His precise date of death is thus uncertain.

Dionysius The Areopagite/Pseudo-Dionysius (c. A.D. 500)
It is commonly assumed that this author was a Syrian Christian monk who adopted the name of Dionysius to give his writings authority (Dionysius the Areopagite was the man Saint Paul converted to Christianity in Athens, recorded in Acts 17:16-34). Little more is known of him except through his works. These show he was indebted to Neoplatonic thought as well as to thinkers such as Gregory of Nyssa and Philo of Alexandria, along with the scriptures. He is the great voice of negative (apophatic) theology, which maintains that one can only say what God is not, not what He is, because God is the ultimate mystery beyond all concepts and words. He was a profound influence on Eckhart, Ruysbroeck, John of the Cross, and others.

Meister Eckhart (1260–1328)
Eckhart is "the father of German mysticism, a profound mystical thinker and a controversial figure whose influence on mystics, theologians, ordinary believers, poets and artists, has continued to this day." When

Eckhart, who was born in central Germany, reached the age of 16 he entered the Dominican order at Erfurt and underwent the usual scholastic training before embarking on a three-year course in theology. In the early 1300s, at about the same time as he completed his studies in Paris and became a Master of Theology (hence the title of "Meister") he was elected head of the new Dominican province of Saxony. He wrote many sermons and treatises expounding his mystical theology, which was deeply influenced by the Neoplatonists and Pseudo-Dionysius. The Ultimate Godhead could never be described or even imagined, and his spiritual advice was to strip away all images or ideas of God, including even the will to do God's will; which prompted a German bishop to accuse him of heresy. Eckhart journeyed to the Pope's Palace in Avignon to plead his case, but he died before hearing the pope's declaration that 17 of his statements were heretical.

T. S. Eliot (1886–1965)
Eliot was born in Missouri. In 1914, with degrees from Harvard, he settled in England, marrying and working as a teacher, and later, in a bank and also as an editor at Faber and Faber. His first book of poems, *Prufrock and Other Observations,* was published in 1917, and immediately established him as the leading poet of the avant-garde. With the publication of *The Waste Land* in 1922, he became the dominant figure in poetry and literary criticism in the English speaking world. In 1927 he became an Anglo-Catholic and a British citizen, and in 1929, in *The Idea of a Christian Society,* he took a controversial stand against the religious pluralism typical of Western democracy. Many other major works followed, including *The Four Quartets* in 1943. He received the 1948 Nobel Prize in Literature.

William Everson (1912–1994)
From early in his adult life Everson, a Californian, was a devotee of the life and work of Robinson Jeffers. During the war, as a conscientious objector, he wrote *The Residual Years,* a volume of poems that launched him into national fame. He joined the Catholic Church in 1948 and took the name of Brother Antoninus on joining the Dominican Order in 1951 in Oakland. He left the Dominicans in 1969 to marry a woman many years his junior. He was stricken by Parkinson's Disease in 1972, and spent the 70s and 80s as poet-in-residence at UC Santa Cruz.

Saint Francis of Assisi (1181–1226)
Francis was the son of a wealthy cloth merchant in the Italian town of Assisi, Umbria. He was on his way south to start a career as a soldier when he heard a voice telling him to return to Assisi. There, while praying in the small church of San Damian outside the city, he heard God say to him, "Go and repair my house because it is falling into ruin." Taking the words literally, Francis sold some of his father's cloth and gave it to the priest of San Damian's. His father was enraged, but Francis

renounced his inheritance and dedicated himself to a life of poverty. In 1208, while attending Mass, he heard a reading from Mathew in which Christ urges his disciples to go out into the world to preach the gospel and heal the sick, and adopt a life of absolute poverty. Francis took the words as a personal summons and immediately acted on them. Others joined him, and the Little Friars came into being; but by 1221 the movement had grown so quickly that the vows of simplicity and poverty were under threat and Francis passed on to others his administrative responsibilities. His most profound mystical experience occurred in 1224 when the stigmata, the five marks of Christ's wounds, appeared on his flesh. Francis did not write about contemplation as such, but his mysticism is to be found in his life: his experience of God existing in all things, and of everything being intimately related through Christ.

Saint Francis de Sales (1567–1622)
Francis was born into a noble family in the duchy of Savoy, between France and Italy, in 1567 at the time of the Wars of Religion. He was educated by the Jesuits in Paris, after which he studied law in Padua. There, he entered the Catholic Church and started a mission to reconvert Calvinist regions back to Catholicism. He became Bishop of Geneva in 1602, and in 1610 he founded the contemplative order of the Visitation for women. For the remaining years of his life he continued his preaching, spiritual direction, and writing (he is the patron saint of writers.) His two spiritual classics are Introduction to *the Devout Life and Treatise on the Love of God*.

Dame Catherine Gascoigne (1600–1676)
Dame Catherine was one of many English Catholics living in exile in Flanders in the mid-1600s. She was abbess of Cambrai Abbey, and taught a form of contemplative prayer that was disapproved of by the authorities, who at the time favored the Jesuit exercises. Catherine's contemplative prayer, inspired by the earlier English mystics, Julian of Norwich, John Tauler, and the author of *The Cloud of Unknowing*, emphasized the unknowability of God and the consequent resting in silence without images. She and her well-known fellow nun, Dame Gertrude More, wrote two inspired and influential works on contemplative prayer as a pathway to mystical union with God.

Kahlil Gibran (1883–1931)
Kahlil Gibran was born into a Christian Maronite family in Lebanon. His father gambled and drank, and eventually ended up in jail, leaving the family poverty-stricken. Gibran consequently had no formal education, but a local priest taught him Arabic and Greek and infused in him an awareness of the mystical dimensions of Maronite Christianity. When he was eight, his mother moved the family to Boston, and Gibran's education began in earnest as the result of a scholarship, revealing early on his gifts for art and poetry. He went to Paris in 1909 to broaden his

art training, and on his return to the States a couple of years later he began to publish Arabic prose poetry through a connection in Egypt, and became active in Arab intellectual and artistic circles in Boston. In 1911 he moved to New York, and it was there that he painted the portrait of Carl Jung. During World War 1 he published *The Prophet*, which has continued to be an international bestseller ever since. He died at the age of 48 of cancer.

Hadewijch of Antwerp (c. 13th century)
Hadewijch was a Flemish Beguine about whom almost nothing is known. The Beguines were lay religious communities of women active in the Low Countries during the 13th and 14th centuries. They took no vows, and lived on the edge of towns, caring for the sick and devoting themselves to contemplation. What was perceived as their quietism often made them vulnerable to charges of heresy. Hadewijch left a body of work consisting of poems, accounts of her visions, and letters to younger Beguines for whom she served as a spiritual guide. These writings were rediscovered only in the 19th century among a cache of medieval manuscripts found in Brussels. She encouraged her charges to trust in their own independent experience, and to remain inwardly detached from whatever circumstance arose in their lives.

Hadewijch II (c. 13th century)
Nothing is known of this Beguine from the Low Countries. In the manuscript of her poetry, her work is seen to have a more apophatic ring than that of Hadewijch of Antwerp, and she was to be an inspiration for later mystics such as Ruysbroeck and Eckhart.

George Herbert (1593–1633)
George Herbert was the most influential of the English Metaphysical poets. Born in Wales into a wealthy family, his father died when George was three. His mother became a great supporter of the arts, and was the patron of John Donne, who started the Metaphysical movement. He wrote his first poems while at Trinity College, Cambridge, saying that the love of God was more worthy a subject for poetry than the love of women, which was a departure from John Donne. He became a well-known university orator, but instead of using his social connections (he was friends with Sir Francis Bacon, among other notable aristocrats) to secure himself a fashionable and profitable position, he decided to become a country parson, and lived for the rest of his life ministering to a small parish in the South West of England. His poems were published after his death in a volume called *The Temple*.

Hildegard of Bingen (1098–1179)
Hildegard was born to a noble German family, and when she was 14 she chose the life of an anchorite (Christian hermit.) At the age of 43,

she became the abbess of a community near Bingen, Saint Rupert's Monastery. Over the course of ten years she wrote an account of her visionary experiences, which was published under the title *Scivias*. She is known to historians through her prodigious correspondence; to mystics for her book of visions; to medical historians and botanists for her two books on natural history and medicine; and to bishops, popes, abbots, and kings. Musicians have also discovered her antiphons, hymns, and a large body of monophonic chants, with text and music both by Hildegard. In her later life, she traveled extensively, preaching to religious and secular clergy.

Geoffrey Hill (1932–)
Hill was born in Worcestershire, England, and published his first collection of poetry at the age of 20 while he was at Keble College Oxford. He has served as Professor of English and Religion at various universities in the UK and the US, retiring finally in 2006 to Cambridge (England) after many years as Professor at Boston University. He has had many volumes of poetry published, and is best known for his dedication to both historical and religious themes. His most recent *Collected Essays* appeared in 2008. While he has received highly favorable critical notice, he is not widely known to the general public, primarily because of the reputed difficulty of his work.

Gerard Manley Hopkins (1844–1889)
Hopkins was born into an Anglican family in 19th-century England. He was educated at Oxford, entered the Catholic Church in 1866, and was ordained a Jesuit priest in 1877. On becoming Catholic, he burned much of his early verse and abandoned the writing of poetry. Then, in 1875, the sinking of a German ship inspired him to write one of his most impressive poems, *The Wreck of the Deutschland,* and he went on to produce his greatest work in the later years of his life. His work was never published during his lifetime, but he has since become recognized as one of the great religious poets of England.

Mark Jarman (1952–)
Jarman was born the oldest of three children in the family of a pastor in Kentucky. His early life was split between California and Scotland, where his father ministered at a number of churches. Poetry was an early love, and at the age of 22 he joined the Iowa Writers Workshop for two years. With Robert McDowell he co-edited *The Reaper,* the primary organ for the New Narrative Poetry Movement, and published his own poetry in a variety of publications. He has gone on to publish nine volumes of poetry, and after teaching at various universities, established his career as Centennial Professor of English at Vanderbilt University in Tennessee. He has received numerous awards and fellowships, and lives with his wife and two children in Nashville.

Jacopone da Todi (1230–1306)

Jacopone Benedetti, known as Jacopone da Todi, was born into a wealthy family in the central Italian town of Todi. As a young man, he married and started a career as a *notario,* combining the skills of an accountant and a lawyer. Legend has it that when a balcony collapsed at a wedding feast, killing his wife, he abandoned his career, gave away all his possessions, and became a wandering penitent. He eventually joined the Franciscan Order, and discovered a gift for poetry. He was imprisoned for five years for his opposition to the election of Pope Boniface VIII, and continued to write deeply personal and mystical poetry in prison. He was released on the death of Boniface, and retired to a hermitage near Orvieto, where he died in 1306.

Julian of Norwich (c. 1342–1420)

Little is known of Julian's life, but it is certain that her life changed for good in 1373 when, after a life-threatening illness, she experienced a series of 16 revelations in the form of visions—mostly of the Passion—and spiritual insights. At some point after this Julian became an anchoress, a hermit dedicated to solitude and prayer, in a cell attached to the Church of Saint Julian in the English city of Norwich. She pondered the visions over the next twenty years, and wrote her reflections on their meaning. At the end of her book, *Revelations of Divine Love,* God tells her the meaning in unambiguous terms: Would you learn your Lord's meaning in this thing? Learn it well; love was his meaning. Who showed it to you? Love. What did he show you? Love. Why did he show it? For love."

Martin Laird

Martin Laird is a Roman Catholic of the Order of Saint Augustine—those charged by Pope John Paul II to be "teachers of the interior life." He is Associate Professor in the Department of Theology and Religious Studies at Villanova University. He has extensive training in contemplative disciplines and gives retreats throughout the United States and Great Britain. He is the translator or author of many books and articles, including *Gregory of Nyssa and the Grasp of Faith* and *Into The Silent Land.*

Denise Levertov (1923–1997)

Soon after emigrating from England to the United States, Levertov was recognized as an important voice in the American avant-garde. Her book *With Eyes at the Back of Our Heads* established her as one of the great American poets, and her English origins were forgotten. She published more than 20 volumes of poetry, and from 1982 to 1993 she taught at Stanford University. She spent the last decade of her life in Seattle, Washington. She was always an outsider, in England, in America, and also in poetry circles, for she never considered herself part of any school.

She once said, "I nevertheless experienced the sense of difference as an honor, as part of knowing (secretly) from an early age—perhaps seven, certainly before I was ten—that I was an artist-person and had a destiny."

Mechtild of Magdeburg (c. 1210–1285)
At the age of 12, Mechtild, the daughter of a wealthy German family, had a defining spiritual experience where she saw "all things in God and God in all things." When she was in her 20s she joined the Beguines, and led a life of simplicity, prayer, and service to the poor. Encouraged by her confessor, she wrote down her mystical experiences over a number of years, completing the work soon after she joined the renowned Cistercian convent of Helfta in Magdeburg, Germany. Her book, *The Flowing Light of the Godhead,* describes the mystical union of lover and beloved, and is considered to be one of the most elevated examples of love poetry in the German language. Dante is said to have based his character Matelda in *Purgatorio* on her.

Thomas Merton (1915–1968)
Merton was a Trappist monk—the most silent of all Catholic orders—poet, and peace activist. In 1947, his autobiography, *The Seven Storey Mountain,* was a surprise best seller and profoundly influenced the immediate postwar interest in monasticism and religion. In the '60s, he became one of the first authoritative Christian voices to take a serious interest in Eastern spirituality, especially Buddhism. He translated Buddhist poets, and in 1968 attended an interfaith meeting of monastic superiors in Bangkok. On that same journey, he met the Dalai Lama in India, and they recognized each other as kindred spirits. Tragically, Merton was accidentally electrocuted in his Bangkok hotel room and died there.

John O'Donohue (1954–2008)
John O'Donohue was an inspiring Irish philosopher, poet, and mystic who lived in the West of Ireland. His native tongue was Gaelic. His Ph.D. dissertation in the field of philosophical theology developed a new concept of Person through a re-interpretation of Hegel. He insisted in his work on beauty as a human calling and a defining aspect of God, and much of his writing drew from pre-Christian and Christian Irish Celtic perspectives. He was well known for his bestselling book *Anam Cara.* In the year of his death his book of blessings, *Benedictus,* was published.

Mary Oliver (1935–)
Mary Oliver is one of America's most widely read contemporary poets. The critic Alicia Ostriker contends that Oliver is "as visionary as Emerson." She won her first poetry prize at the age of 27, from the Poetry Society of America, for her collection *No Voyage.* She won the Pulitzer

Prize in 1984 for her collection of poems *American Primitive*, and she was winner of the 1992 National Book Award for poetry for her *New and Selected Poems*. Her more recent work continues to evoke a reverence for the natural world and also reflects the influence of her entry into the Christian faith in 2005. In 2008 three of her newest collections were in the top five of the Poetry Bestseller list compiled by Book Sense.

Saint Paul (c. 5–67)
Paul, known as Saul before his conversion, was the son of a Roman citizen in a wealthy Jewish family in Tarsus. He was sent to rabbinical school in Jerusalem, where, along with his studies, he learned the art of tent-making. In AD 35 he was virulently anti-Christian, and believed the new sect should be wiped out. On his way to Damascus to protest against the Christians there, he was struck blind. On arriving in Damascus he experienced a sudden conversion, and was cured of his blindness by the disciple Ananias, and then baptized. He was called to preach the Gospel, but he felt unworthy and retired for three years to the desert to meditate and pray. Then followed the most extraordinary life of preaching, writing and church-founding all around the Mediterranean. He was finally martyred in Jerusalem.

Marguerite Porete (d. 1310)
Marguerite was a Beguine, the lay-women renunciates in the Low Countries. Her radical faith is described in her book *Mirror of Simple Souls*, in which she refers contemptuously to the established church as Sainte Église la Petite (Little Holy Church) and contrasted it to the Great Holy Church of those "annihilated in God." Accused of the heresy of the Free Spirit movement (the belief that once the soul has reached maturity it is beyond all moral conventions and any need of the sacraments or the Church as an intermediary between itself and God), Marguerite was publicly burned at the stake in Paris on June 1, 1310. During the year and a half she was in prison before her death, she refused to say a word to her Inquisitor.

Rainer Maria Rilke (1875–1926)
Rilke survived a lonely and unhappy childhood in Prague to publish his first volume of poetry, *Leben und Lieder,* in 1894. In 1896 he left Prague for the University of Munich. In 1902 in Paris he became friend and secretary to the sculptor Rodin, and the next 12 years in Paris saw his greatest poetic activity. In 1919 he moved to Switzerland, where he wrote his last two works, *Sonnets to Orpheus* and *Duino Elegies*. He died in Switzerland of leukemia in 1926. His reputation has grown enormously since his death, and he is now considered one of the greatest poets of the 20th century.

Blessed John Ruysbroeck (1293–1381)
Ruysbroeck was born in the village near Brussels for which he was named. As a child he went to live with his uncle, a canon in Brussels,

who educated him. In 1317 he entered the priesthood and was a prebend at the cathedral for 26 years, living a simple, austere life and speaking out against the heretical Brethren of the Free Spirit, who were active in the area at the time. When he was 50 years old he left Brussels with his uncle to pursue a contemplative life in the forest. They soon attracted disciples and eventually created a community of Augustinian canons. For the rest of his life Ruysbroeck immersed himself in his mystical writings and giving counsel to the many visitors who sought him out. His best known work is *The Adornment of the Spiritual Marriage*, which shows the influence of the Eckhart school of negative theology. He is generally acknowledged to be the greatest Flemish contemplative.

Angelus Silesius (1624–1677)
Angelus Silesius was the monastic name of Johannes Scheffler, who was born into a noble Polish Lutheran family. He received a doctorate from the University of Padua and became a physician. As a young man he was drawn to the writings of the German mystic, Jakob Böhme. His own growing mysticism was more suited to Catholicism than his native faith, and he converted in 1653. In 1661 he was ordained a priest and retired to monastic life in Breslau, giving away his family fortune to charities. He wrote two books of poetry, *The Soul's Spiritual Delight* and *The Cherubic Pilgrim*. He was disapproved of by the church authorities because his poetry suggested that the soul, in deep quiet, could experience God directly.

Saint Symeon the New Theologian (949–1022)
Saint Symeon is one of the most beloved of saints in the Christian Orthodox Church. He is one of only three great Fathers who have been granted the title of Theologian by the Church, because he is one of a very few in the history of Christianity who is considered to have "known God." Theology, in the Orthodox tradition, is considered to spring from direct revelation rather than from study and learning. Saint Symeon's whole teaching was of the availability of a personal experience of the living Christ. His writings, which are easily available today, grew out of his preaching and spiritual directions to the monks who were in his charge. He is still eagerly read by Orthodox monks and is finding an increasing audience in Roman monasteries, too.

Paula Tatarunis
Paula Tatarunis is a poet, Episcopalian, trinitarian universalist, and a weed photographer. She practices medicine in the Boston area. "November 1938" appears as the text of a movement of the Jazz Oratorio, *The Death Of Simone Weil*, by composer Darrell Katz, issued by Innova Records.

John Tauler (1300–1361)
Tauler was born in Strasburg, and remained there most of his life. He was educated at the local Dominican convent and subsequently spent his life preaching and acting as a spiritual director to Dominican nuns.

During the Black Death epidemic of 1348 he ministered tirelessly to the sick. Tauler's sermons speak of the birth of God in the soul, and like his mentor, Eckhart, Tauler often used the image of the desert and a place of unfathomable darkness and invisible light to convey the ineffability of God. He saw the contemplative and the active life to be mutually supportive of each other and often said it was not necessary to become a monk or a priest to know God.

Theophan the Recluse (1815–1891)
Theophan was born in a village in the heart of Russia, and his father was a priest. He attended Kiev Theological Academy, and then held various teaching posts at seminaries, but this did not satisfy him, and he asked to be relieved of academic service. In 1859 he was made Bishop of Tambov, but an administrative life in the world was not suited to his contemplative nature, and in 1866 he was allowed to retire to Vysha Hermitage, where he stayed for the rest of his life, absorbed in perpetual prayer. He received 20 to 40 letters daily and replied to all of them with deep spiritual counsel. He wrote many books, including *What Is Spiritual Life?* His practice was to dwell on God in his heart at all times, whatever he was doing.

R.S. Thomas (1913–2000)
Thomas was the pre-eminent Welsh poet of the 20th century. A fervent Welsh nationalist who learned the Welsh language, he nevertheless wrote all his poetry in English. Born in Cardiff and educated at the University College of North Wales, he was ordained as an Anglican priest in 1936 and spent his working life as a clergyman in rural Wales. He wrote about faith, nature, the Welsh countryside, and the landscapes within in more than 20 volumes of poetry. His *Collected Poems 1945–1990* was published in 1993. In 1964, he was awarded the Queen's Gold Medal for Poetry, and at the end of his life he was nominated for the Nobel Prize. His international standing rests primarily on the quality of his religious poetry.

The Gospel of Thomas (c. 1st century)
The Gospel of Thomas was first identified as a Coptic manuscript forming part of the Nag Hammadi Library discovered in 1945. The text, which consists of 114 sayings attributed to Jesus, identifies the author as Didymos Judas Thomas the Apostle, though it was a common practice in the early centuries after Christ for a writer to attribute his works to one of the Apostles, and the authorship has not been authenticated. The orthodox church condemned this and other apocryphal texts as Gnostic heresies, and the Gospel of Thomas in particular was criticized as being the work of the Manichaean sect. Current scholarship suggests it was written much earlier than originally thought, probably a few decades after the death of Christ.

Henry Vaughan (1621–1695)

Vaughan was one of the best-known English Metaphysical poets. Born in Wales into a prosperous family, he went to Oxford along with his twin brother, Thomas, who later became an alchemist and hermetic philosopher. Henry had a powerful mystical conversion which he attributed to the inspired poetry of George Herbert, though he himself was more mystical in tone. His poetry describes ecstatic states of communion with the divine and a deep affinity for the natural world. He became a physician, and married in 1646, the same year his first volume of poetry was published. In 1650 the first part of his greatest work, *The Fiery Flint*, was published.

Simone Weil (1909–1943)

Simone Weil was born into an agnostic Jewish family in Paris. In her early teens she mastered Greek and several modern languages. In 1928 she finished first in the entrance exam for France's most prestigious school, l'École Normale Supérieure. She went on to alternate teaching philosophy with manual labor in factories and fields, and shared her salary with the unemployed. After witnessing the horrors of the Spanish Civil War, she expressed her disillusionment with ideologies, and in the mid-1930s she became increasingly drawn to Christianity. Though refusing to be baptized, she converted from Judaism in 1938, and began to have mystical experiences. In England during the Second World War she worked for de Gaulle's Free French Movement. She died at the age of 34 of tuberculosis and self neglect—she refused food and medical treatment out of sympathy for the people of occupied France. During her life she published only a few poems and articles. With her posthumous works—16 volumes—she earned a reputation as one of the most original thinkers of her era. T.S. Eliot called her "a woman of genius, a kind of genius akin to that of the saints."

permissions

further reading

The most valuable resource I found in researching this book was the Website: **poetry-chaikhana.com**.
A treasure trove of spiritual poetry from all traditions.

Into The Silent Land. Martin Laird.
An excellent and lyrically written primer on the Christian contemplative life by a contemporary retreat leader.

Love Burning in the Soul. James Harpur.
An invaluable introduction to the tradition of Christian mysticism over two thousand years.

Christian Mystics of the Middle Ages. Ed. Paul de Jaecher
Excerpts from the original work of some of the great saints.

Christian Mystics: Their Lives and Legacies Throughout the Ages.
Ursula King
Sixty profiles of men and women across the ages who exemplify the mystical life.

about the author

Roger Housden is the author of 17 books, including the Ten Poems series, as well as *Seven Sins for a Life Worth Living; Dancing with Joy; Risking Everything; How Rembrandt Reveals Your Beautiful, Imperfect Self; Chasing Rumi;* and *Sacred Journeys in a Modern World.* Housden is a respected lecturer who presents in both the private and corporate arenas on the transformational power of poetry and living a life of meaning. His work has been featured many times in *O, The Oprah Magazine; The New York Times;* and the *Los Angeles Times.* He has written feature articles for *The Guardian* newspaper and has been an interviewer for BBC radio. Roger resides in Marin County, California.

Website: **www.rogerhousden.com**

Hay House Titles of Related Interest

YOU CAN HEAL YOUR LIFE, the movie,
starring Louise Hay & Friends
(available as a 1-DVD program and an expanded 2-DVD set)
Watch the trailer at: **www.LouiseHayMovie.com**

THE SHIFT, the movie,
starring Dr. Wayne W. Dyer
(available as a 1-DVD program and an expanded 2-DVD set)
Watch the trailer at: **www.DyerMovie.com**

RETURN TO THE SACRED:
Ancient Pathways to Spiritual Awakening,
by Jonathan H. Ellerby, Ph.D.

SAVED BY A POEM: The Transformative Power of Words,
by Kim Rosen

WRITING IN THE SAND: Jesus & the Soul of the Gospels,
by Thomas Moore

All of the above are available at your local bookstore,
or may be ordered by contacting Hay House (see next page).

We hope you enjoyed this Hay House book. If you'd like to receive our online catalog featuring additional information on Hay House books and products, or if you'd like to find out more about the Hay Foundation, please contact:

Hay House, Inc., P.O. Box 5100, Carlsbad, CA 92018-5100
(760) 431-7695 or (800) 654-5126
(760) 431-6948 (fax) or (800) 650-5115 (fax)
www.hayhouse.com® • **www.hayfoundation.org**

Published and distributed in Australia by: Hay House Australia Pty. Ltd., 18/36 Ralph St., Alexandria NSW 2015 • *Phone:* 612-9669-4299 *Fax:* 612-9669-4144 • www.hayhouse.com.au

Published and distributed in the United Kingdom by: Hay House UK, Ltd., Astley House, 33 Notting Hill Gate, London W11 3JQ *Phone:* 44-20-3675-2450 • *Fax:* 44-20-3675-2451 www.hayhouse.co.uk

Published and distributed in the Republic of South Africa by: Hay House SA (Pty), Ltd., P.O. Box 990, Witkoppen 2068 *Phone/Fax:* 27-11-467-8904 • www.hayhouse.co.za

Published in India by: Hay House Publishers India, Muskaan Complex, Plot No. 3, B-2, Vasant Kunj, New Delhi 110 070 • *Phone:* 91-11-4176-1620 • *Fax:* 91-11-4176-1630 • www.hayhouse.co.in

Distributed in Canada by: Raincoast Books, 2440 Viking Way, Richmond, B.C. V6V 1N2 *Phone:* 1-800-663-5714 • *Fax:* 1-800-565-3770 • www.raincoast.com

---

<u>Take Your Soul on a Vacation</u>

Visit **www.HealYourLife.com®** to regroup, recharge, and reconnect with your own magnificence. Featuring blogs, mind-body-spirit news, and life-changing wisdom from Louise Hay and friends.

Visit **www.HealYourLife.com** today!

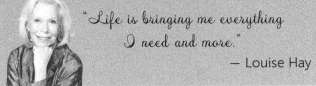

CPSIA information can be obtained
at www.ICGtesting.com
Printed in the USA
LVHW111735210421
685071LV00003B/6

9 781401 923877